SEEDS FOR THE SOUL

*This book is dedicated to my mother Mary Rose McGuire
and my late father Daniel McGuire
who have always been an inspiration to me
as to how to walk the path of life with eyes of faith.
They have showed me how the seeds of faith can be nourished
and brought to fruit.*

Brendan McGuire

Seeds for the Soul

SUNDAY HOMILIES FOR
CYCLE C

God Bless

Fr. Brendan

the columba press

First published in 2003 by
the columba press
55A Spruce Avenue, Stillorgan Industrial Park,
Blackrock, Co Dublin

Cover by Bill Bolger
Origination by The Columba Press
Printed in Ireland by ColourBooks Ltd, Dublin

ISBN 1 85607 420 X

Acknowledgements
The author and publishers are grateful to Paulist Press, Mahwah, New
Jersey for permission to quote from *The Sower's Seeds, Sower's Seeds
Aplenty* and *Fresh Packet of Sower's Seeds* by Brian Cavanaugh, and to
Tyndale House Publishers, Wheaten, Illinois, for permission to quote
from *Illustrations Unlimited* by James S. Hewett. Other sources of inspir-
ation are noted in the footnotes throughout the book and are listed in
the author's acknowledgements on page 7.
Scripture quotations are taken from *The New Revised Standard Version*,
copyright (c) 1989, by the Division of Christian Education of the
National Council of the Churches of Christ in the United States of
America. Used by permission.

Contents

Introduction

I have always believed that God's ways are mysterious yet understandable, hidden yet knowable, divine yet human. In the struggle to understand God's ways we need to reflect on his role in our lives. The only way we experience life is through our fragile human ways and so it is in the ordinariness of life, I believe, that God speaks to us. He speaks loudly yet clearly if 'we have ears to hear'.

The title of this book was inspired by the Parable of the Sower of seeds in Matthew 13. The seed of the Word of God is proclaimed every week at Mass throughout the world and yet we still do not fully understand the power of God's Word in our lives. My humble attempt in this book of homilies is to relate the proclaimed Word to the every day life of the person hearing the proclaimed Word. Many of these homilies were proclaimed to a community of faith in Santa Clara, California and relate to their lives.

My hope is that the reader of this book can find a place in their soul to plant the seed of God through these stories, and somewhere on the journey through life allow God to water this seed and bring it to fruition. May God bless your reflection and the 'planting of the seed'.

Acknowledgements
Every week for the last three years since my ordination to priesthood I wrote out my homily for the Sunday Mass. Then, after I had edited it several times, I sent the homily via electronic mail to a list of friends and family who had requested it. One of those friends, Audry Lynch, an author herself, asked me to consider collecting my weekly homilies and getting them published. She then put me in contact with The Columba Press. To Audry, I thank you for your encouragement and confidence in these homilies. Thank you to Seán O Boyle and Brian Lynch for their patience with this novice author.

I have drawn on the following books for inspiration and ideas in preparing these homilies: *Only Jesus Always Jesus* by Socrates B. Vellegas (Anvil, Philippines), *Who Told You that You Were Naked?* by John Jacob Raub (Crossroads, NY), *Celebration:*

An Ecumenical Worship Resource (NCR, Kansas, MO), *Lent: The Daily Readings* by Megan McKenna (Orbis, NY), *The Word among Us: Lent* by Megan McKenna (Orbis, NY), *Biblical Meditations for Lent* by Carroll Stuhlmueller (Paulist, NJ), *Fresh Packet of Sower's Seeds* by Brian Cavanaugh (Paulist, NJ), *Like Fresh Bread* by Robert Waznak (Paulist, NJ), *Sower's Seeds Aplenty* by Brian Cavanaugh (Paulist, NJ), *Tell the Next Generation* by William Burghardt (Paulist, NJ), *The Sower's Seeds* by Brian Cavanaugh (Paulist, NJ), *Homily Helps* (St Anthony Messenger Press, OH), *Preachers Exchange* by Jude Siciliano (Raleigh, NC: preachex@op-south.org), *Grace upon Grace* by William F. Maestri (St Paul, Philippines), *Action 2000 – Cycle C* by Mark Link (Tabor, TX), *Preaching the Lectionary* by Reginald H. Fuller (Liturgical Press, MN), *Storytelling the Word* and *Timely Homilies* by William J. Bausch (Twenty-Third, CT), *Illustrations Unlimited* by James S. Hewett (Tyndale House, Ill),

Nearly every week I 'bounce' my ideas for the homily off friends to help create just the right message. For three years Sr Kathleen Hanley, RSM and Jed DeTorres have listened patiently, critiqued gently and suggested strongly to my ideas. My gratitude to them for their patience, kindness and inspiration since their wisdom is embedded within these homilies.

I also want to thank the parishioners of St Lawrence the Martyr Parish, Santa Clara, California for their support over the last three years, giving me inspiration by their display of faith. In a special way I want to acknowledge John Jabin and Steve Varnau who pushed me to complete the text for publishing and enabled me to do so by proof-reading each homily and doing the final edits. Without their help this book would not have been a reality.

Finally I want to thank my closest brother Paul and his wife Maria and their two children Daniella and Dominic who are the source of great love and truly the source of inspiration for so many homilies. Their friendship and love sustains me from week to week. Thank you.

Promise to Return

The most celebrated American in the Philippines is General Douglas MacArthur. Most Filipinos not only know his name but genuinely celebrate it as one of their own. Several summers ago I visited there and was perplexed by this fame. On Corregidor island there is a large monument of MacArthur, probably 20-30 feet tall. In Leyte there is a life size depiction, carved in metal, of his landing on the beach. You see, during World War II General MacArthur was stationed in the Philippines but he had to leave to fight in Japan. Before leaving he promised his return to the Filipino people saying, 'I will return.' Several months later he did return with a large contingent of soldiers and rescued the Philippines from occupation by the Japanese. MacArthur was their hero!

The most celebrated man in the Western world is Jesus Christ and he promised his return when he knew his death was imminent. In today's gospel we hear Luke depict a dramatic return of the Messiah.

This reading is a continuation of the apocalyptic literature of Luke. It is a unique form of literature, characterised by extreme images and strange creatures. The intention of this literature was to address a suffering people and help them look beyond the present moment of grief to a longed-for time of peace and justice.

This gospel is trying to inspire us to lead a life of holiness and to always expect Christ to be with us and to save us in times of trouble.

Today we celebrate the first Sunday of Advent. Each year we celebrate this time of year by decorating the church with purple, the ancient colour of anticipation. We have an Advent wreath and light one candle each week, lighting the way of the Lord.

The church asks us to focus on the three ways that Christ comes. He came in history 2000 years ago when Jesus was born as the Son of Mary and Son of God. He comes now with the gift of the Holy Spirit which dwells within us. He comes again in glory at the end of time. He will judge the living and the dead.

That was Christ's promise to us: He will return. The question

9

that we can ask ourselves this week is: If Christ was really to return this coming Christmas, are we ready? If Christ was really to arrive in judgement, have we prepared ourselves? This week may we prepare ourselves in some small way so that this Christmas can be about the arriving of Christ within us.

We need to prepare our hearts for Christ and often blame remains in our heart. Reconciliation is one way to prepare our hearts for the Lord. For some of us this could be reconciling with an old friend we have fallen out with. For others of us this could be reconciliation with a family member. For some of us at school this may be trying harder to be a good boy or girl. Whatever it is, may we make a promise to prepare ourselves in some small way this week by reconciling with someone. Then we can be ready for his promise: 'I will return.'

Highway to God

When I was home in Ireland this summer I was amazed by the amount of new construction. There were houses and office buildings going up everywhere! One thing in particular struck me – the number of new roads and highways.[1]

When I grew up, there were no highways in Ireland at all. Now we have lots of them and more under construction. Near my home town there is one such highway. Before the highway existed the land was covered in hills and valleys and the old roads were twisted. Now it is a straight and wide highway! They filled in the valleys, levelled the hills and generally made the path wide and straight. Now we can travel at fast speeds from one place to another and can get to our destination faster.

A similar thing happened here with the building of Highway 85.[2] When I first arrived here, 14 years ago, there was no highway. It was a twisted road too! Then they levelled the hills and filled in the valleys. In our case it was the levelling of houses too as this highway made its way through major cities. And now we have a straight and wide highway connecting South San Jose, Los Gatos, Cupertino and Mountain View. We can travel at fast speeds from one place to another – we get to our destination faster.

We hear in today's gospel John the Baptist fulfilling the prophecy of the prophet Isaiah. He was preparing the way of the Lord, clearing him a straight path, filling in the valleys and levelling the mountain.

John proclaimed the gospel by calling Israel to God's vision for them. He called them to repent and listen to the gospel. He told them that they were the chosen race and were destined to receive the Messiah into their midst. John was preparing the way for the Messiah, Christ Jesus.

He persisted in his understanding of God's vision. How do we understand God's vision for us? How are we preparing the way for the Lord in our lives? God's vision for us, as scripture tells us, is that we are his children. We are called to be his adopted children and heirs to his eternal kingdom.

God came to earth in his Son, Jesus Christ and gave redemption to all of humanity. We are now invited to God's offer of salvation by accepting his call to discipleship.

This Advent season we are called to prepare the way for the Lord in accordance with God's vision for all of us. What hills are in our hearts that need to be levelled? Maybe we have an old grudge that needs forgiving. Maybe there is someone at work or at school with whom we find it difficult to be in the same room. Or maybe we have not talked with some relative for a long time. We are called to level that hill.

What valley needs filling in? Maybe it is to spend a little more time in prayer (just 10 minutes a day). Or maybe we could do some act of charity for someone in real need such as participating in the Giving Tree[3] and giving to children in need. Maybe we can do something we feel God is calling us to do at home with our family or neighbours. Whatever it is, we are called to fill in that valley!

There are many other ways we can prepare the way for the Lord according to his vision for us as children of God. You can think of more than I have suggested but we are called to build highways for God in our hearts and in the hearts of those around us so our communication with God is clearer. Today let us build a highway to God.

---

1. Highways are what Americans call Motorways.
2. Highway 85 is located in San Jose, California and connects five major cities through densely populated districts. It was very controversial when under construction.
3. The 'Giving Tree' or 'Jesse Tree' is a Christmas tree placed in the vestibule of the church with tags asking for donated gifts for children in need. Our parish community usually supplies over 500 gifts for needy children.

Pregnant with Christ!

This is the season of Advent, a preparation time for Christmas. When we started the Mass we sang *O Come Emmanuel* and Emmanuel means God-is-with-us. And that is what we celebrate in Advent – God with us.

Yet from the beginning of our shared history as a people of God of faith, we have always been assured of God's presence, that God is with us. When God forged a covenant with Abraham, renewed again with Isaac and Moses, with all the prophets, the message was the same, 'I am with you.'

So what is so different in the message we hear today? The difference, I suggest, is that in becoming one of us, God is with us in every way, in every aspect of human experience, in every adventure we take, in every sorrow we endure. In Jesus, God has pioneered a new way for us to follow. In Jesus, God is within every person through 'the abiding indwelling presence of the Holy Spirit.' (Rom 8:9, Jn 14:15-17)

So how do we joyfully realise that gift of his presence? At this point I would like to try a little experiment in imagination. It's a little risky but let's give it a try. I want everybody, the boys, girls, women, and men to try this. And I know that you boys and men will have a difficult time with this. But just give it a try!

Let us close our eyes and imagine ourselves pregnant with Christ like Mary was pregnant with Jesus. As we think of the Christ within us, what size is Christ? What month do we think we are in our pregnancy? Is it the first month and really nobody can tell that Christ lives within except yourself? Or are we in the ninth month and we quite obviously are giving birth to someone within? Okay you can open your eyes now.

I suggest that we ought to be like Mary at this point: it is only a few days from the birth of Jesus and she is very pregnant indeed. Are we that pregnant and if not, we need to ask why not. In others words, does the Christ within us show through to others? Can people tell we are Christians by the way we love others? Can everyone see how unselfish we are, as the letter to Philippians puts it today?

Well, maybe this Christmas we can make a special effort to accept with great joy in our hearts the Christ within us. Maybe we can show the Christ within us to others and recognise the Christ within others.

The gospel today gives us some ways to prepare for the Lord in our hearts. Let the person who has two cloaks give to others that have none. May we share what we have with those around us – our money and time. Like those tax collectors maybe we ought to take only what we need. We are called not to be greedy this season but share all we have.

Like the soldiers we ought not to bully others. We are called to be patient and kind, especially with the very old and very young.

These are suggestions from today's gospel. There are many more we can think of.

Whatever it is, let us look for those opportunities these last few days to display the Christ within. May we not wait passively for Christ to return but eagerly look for opportunities to show Christ to others. May we show the Christ within us to others this week before Christmas by acting in ways that Jesus would. Then I think we can say that God is *in us* as well as God is *with us*.

Doing the Ordinary
and Letting God Do the Extraordinary

Many of you will recognise today's gospel scene as the second joyful mystery of the rosary, the Visitation. I am sure most of you have seen paintings or carving depicting the visitation of Elizabeth by Mary, from Michelangelo to Raphael. I have even received Christmas cards with this very scene.[1]

You have noticed that most of these depictions have both Mary and Elizabeth dressed in royal robes, embracing each other in a regal manner. However, the reality is that they were two peasant women who journeyed on foot, sharing their hopes and dreams with each other. One was a barren old woman and the other a young girl.

This is where God chose to make his kingdom become a reality. He chose ordinary women. He did not choose royalty. He did not choose heroes. But they have become our royalty, they have become our heroes in the faith.

Today, if we want to know whom we consider our heroes we can go to the newspaper stands and see who the tabloid magazines are talking about. Those heroes are most often the rich and famous – actors or actresses, sports stars or famous wealthy people. We might be inclined to believe that if God chose someone from one of these higher social ranks as the mother of the 'royal' Son then Jesus might have been more readily accepted. Isn't that how we rank one another, by profession, education, social status, etc.?

But God's ways are very different. He chose a simple young girl and an old barren woman, both of simple faith and trust in God. They are not chosen because they are wealthy or famous or even from royal stock. God chose them as ordinary people who did ordinary things and he did the extraordinary with them. They are our unlikely heroes!

Our children's stories are full of unlikely heroes. They often keep the story of our faith alive. For example, think of Cinderella. She is the ordinary girl who does all the ordinary duties of the house. But her moment of glory comes when she goes to the dance. She is the one that the extraordinary happens to.

She becomes the centre of the story because of her ordinary yet beautiful self.

Many children's stories mirror the gospel story of unlikely heroes. God chooses all of us to be unlikely heroes in the faith. God chooses each one of us as ordinary folk, to be extraordinary by our actions in faith. And God gives us role models in faith such as Mary to learn from.

Mary is ordinary insofar as she lived life in an ordinary place and did the ordinary duties of every day life. Yet she is extraordinary insofar as she is obedient and gives herself into God's hands. She is willing to take risks, for she trusts God. Mary did the ordinary things of life but with an extraordinary faith and trust in God.[2] We are called to follow Mary's example of faith.

This last Sunday of Advent, and indeed this Christmas, we are called to do the ordinary things of life with a simple faith and trust in God. I believe if we do the ordinary things of life well then God will make them extraordinary. That is our act of faith.

Maybe like Mary in today's gospel we are called to go and see a relative who needs a visit. Maybe we are called to write a letter to a distant friend so as to connect again. Or maybe we are invited to spend some time with our own family for whom we normally find it difficult to find time.

We are called to the ordinary and God will make it extraordinary. Today it is with us that God chooses to make his kingdom become a reality. May we be the new unlikely heroes of faith by doing the ordinary things of life with joy and peace in our hearts, knowing that God will do the extraordinary.

1. Jude Siciliano, OP, 'Preachers Exchange,' (Raleigh, NC: preachex@opsouth.org).
2. *Celebration: An Ecumenical Worship Resource*, (Kansas City, MO: National Catholic Reporter Company, Inc., December, 2000).

Hidden Christ Among Us!

It was December 17, 1976 and we had just finished decorating the house for Christmas. It was our family custom that all the children help decorate the house on December 17. Suddenly and loudly, the doorbell rang late into the evening. It was the regular beggar who came every Saturday to ask my mother for money. But it was Tuesday and she was here for her 'Christmas bonus'. She boldly stood at the door and asked, 'Howaye son, can ye tell yur mother Mrs O'Brien is here.' I stood defiant and replied, 'My mother is out' – my usual answer! She quickly retorted, 'Ah yeah, but could you please tell her anyway. I'll wait here, thanks very much.' And as if by divine command I turned and told my mum that the old beggar was here again. Much to my chagrin, my mother took two pounds (about $5) out of her purse and gave it to Mrs O'Brien after having a little conversation with her. Two pounds was a lot of money to an eleven-year old, especially in a house of twelve children where the best gift I would get that Christmas would be hand-me-down clothes or my own box of cornflakes. Since all the money exchanged between the children came from my parents, I saw the two pounds as taken directly from my pocket.

As soon as the door closed I immediately questioned my mother. 'Do you know that Mrs. O'Brien never begs at any other house on the street? Nobody else gives her anything, because she's a fraud. And as long as you keep giving her money she will keep coming back. Why did you give her so much, anyway?' My mother responded ever so casually, 'Because she needed it and I had it to give.' I'll never forget that lesson and I never turned Mrs O'Brien away again. That year my mother's best Christmas gift was her example of charity, showing me how to see Christ hidden beneath the guise of a beggar.

The shepherds in Bethlehem of today's gospel got a hidden message. They were to see a child lying in a manger. This child would be their King and their Messiah. Hidden message indeed!

They had to look beyond the outward appearances to see the real message. They had to see that this little vulnerable infant was indeed their Messiah. In the same way my mother had to

look beyond the outward appearance of the old beggar, Mrs
O'Brien. She was able to see the Christ that lived within Mrs
O'Brien. Such a simple act of charity carries a lot of weight.

There are many hidden messages to Christmas but the primary one is that Christ lives among us here and now. He dwells
within each of us today. While we may not see angels who give
us direct messages, we do celebrate Christ's incarnation and
birthday. We also celebrate his presence among us now.

Within whom in our lives can we seek the hidden Christ this
week? Can we tend to the hidden Christ in those around us?
May we be like the shepherds of this morning's gospel or like
my mom, and not only see the Christ who lives among us but
care for and give to the hidden Christ. There is always someone
in whom we have not seen the Christ. Who is it this Christmas?

Christmas: Dawn Mass:
Is 62:11-12; Tit 3:4-7; Lk 2:15-20

The Hidden Message of Christmas: Believing, Seeing, and Acting

The shepherds returned, glorifying and praising God for all they had heard and seen, in accord with what had been told them.

Since November Christmas music has filled the air of the shops and the department stores. I imagine that the people who work at the checkout counters are relieved that Christmas is finally here.Have you ever noticed the lyrics of those songs and wondered where they came from or if they have a hidden meaning? Well some do! 'The Twelve Days of Christmas', for example, was written in sixteenth-century England.

Actually it was written by a couple of crafty Jesuits who were playing a dangerous game. In sixteenth-century England anything Catholic was prohibited. If discovered it was punishable by imprisonment or death. As a result, the Catholic faith was forced underground. Still, there was a desperate need to encourage the faith and pass the faith on to the next generation.

These Jesuits came up with a way to teach an outline of the faith – but in code. The code is our song. Here is the code decoded: The Twelve Days of Christmas were the days from the Nativity celebration of Christmas Day to Epiphany. 'My true love gave to me' is God speaking to the anonymous Catholic. The 'twelve drummers drumming' are not, as you might guess, the twelve apostles, but rather the twelve beliefs outlined in the Apostles' Creed. The 'eleven pipers piping' are the eleven apostles – Judas having left – who pipe the faith in an unbroken tradition. The 'ten lords a-leaping' are the Ten Commandments. The 'nine ladies dancing' are the nine choirs of angels. The 'eight maids a-milking' are the eight beatitudes. The 'seven swans a-swimming' are the seven sacraments. The 'six geese a-laying' are the six precepts of the church. The 'five golden rings' are the first five books of the Bible, called the Torah. The 'four calling birds' are the four gospels that sing the good news. The 'three French hens' are the three gifts of the Magi. The 'two turtle doves' are the Old and New Testaments. And finally 'the partridge in a pear tree' is the resplendent Christ reigning from the cross. Now for the uninitiated sixteenth-century English Protestant, the song was a simple holiday pleasantry. But for those who were playing hide-and-seek with their faith, it was a coded outline from which they could unfold the truths of faith, a kind of catechism with chapter headings that teachers could secretly use to hang their teachings on.

People have always used imaginative ways to pass on the faith and to restate the basic gospel message, especially the message of Christmas. Luke certainly did with his story of the shepherds and choir of angels. Our Christmas gospel today is not about the flutter of angels and their music. Luke tells us they've gone back to heaven. The story is about simple folk, shepherds who see with their eyes of faith and act by going to Bethlehem. They are the forerunners, not of the apostles, but of future believers who will glorify God for what they have heard and praise God for what they have seen. They believed first, saw what they believed and then acted on what they saw.

I am sure we received the tradition of our faith in all sorts of different ways. Some were probably hidden like the lyrics of the song and the shepherds in the gospel. Maybe they were hidden in the way a teacher taught us or the way a sports coach coached us. Maybe it was the way our parents or grandparents guided us in the faith by sharing their own life of faith.

We are called to believe first and look at life with faith and then act on what we see. Today we acknowledge our faith by our presence at church. May we look back and see the many ways we received our faith and act on that gift of faith. As dawn breaks on this Christmas morning we approach the holy table to celebrate another hiddenness – the mystery of Christ's birth.

We believe in the presence of Jesus here and we are challenged to see Jesus shining in and through our neighbour. We are called to act upon what we see and give glory and praise to God.

The shepherds returned, glorifying and praising God for all they had heard and seen, in accord with what had been told them.

Christmas: Day Mass:
Is 52:7-10; Heb 1:1-6; Jn 1:1-18

God Dwells Among Us

In the beginning was the Word...
and the Word was God...
The Word became flesh and made his dwelling among us.

Once upon a cold Christmas Eve, a man sat in reflective silence before the flames flickering in the fireplace, thinking about the meaning of Christmas. 'There is no point to a God who became human,' he thought. 'Why would an all-powerful God want to share even one moment as one of us? And even if he did, why would God choose to be born in a stable? No way! The whole thing is absurd! If God wanted to become one of us he would have found another way; a simpler and more direct way.' Then suddenly the man was roused from his thoughts by a strange sound outside. He sprang to the window and quickly gazed outside. He saw a gaggle of snow geese frantically honking and wildly flapping their wings amid the deep snow and frigid cold. They seemed dazed and confused. Apparently, due to exhaustion, they dropped out of a larger flock migrating to a warmer climate.

Moved to compassion, the man bundled up and went outside. He opened up his garage and tried to shoo the shivering geese into it, but the more he shooed, the more the geese panicked. 'If they only realised that I'm trying to save them,' he thought to himself. 'How can I make them understand my concern for their well-being?'

Then a thought came to him: 'If for just one minute, I could become one of them, if I could become a snow goose and communicate with them in their own language, then they would know what I'm trying to do.'

In that flash of inspiration, he remembered it was Christmas Eve. The Christmas story no longer seemed absurd.[1]

In today's gospel we hear 'the Word became flesh and dwelt among us.' Our loving father in heaven became one of us in Jesus. Today we celebrate the incarnation of God. Today we celebrate that God put flesh on and became like us. In the same way as the man wanting to communicate to the geese, God

wanted to communicate directly with us and so he became one
of us. He communicated with us in our own language in order
for us to understand that he was trying to save us. He wanted
the world to be reconciled with God and with one and another.
God gave life to his words and dwelt among us!

In the Jewish tradition when someone spoke something they
gave the words life. Thus when God spoke his words they had
life. His breath gave life. All our breaths give life. For this reason
Jews, even to this day, do not speak the Lord's name because
they would not dare to presume to give life to God.

Our words give life too. Sometimes we may say something
we do not intend and it's too late. The damage has been done
and we cannot take back the words. During the Christmas season we sometimes find that those hurts, from words previously
said, are still there. Whether we said the words ourselves or
whether they were said to us, we still feel the pain.

God gave life to Christ by his spoken word in order that we
be reconciled with one another. Today we can recognise Christ
again by speaking words of reconciliation. Let us choose just one
person whom we can be reconciled with and so make the living
Christ be more alive this year in our lives.

In the beginning was the Word...
and the Word was God...
The Word became flesh and made his dwelling among us.

1. Brian Cavanagh, *Fresh Packet of Sower's Seeds*, (Mahwah, New Jersey:
Paulist Press, 1994) #67.

Feast of The Holy Family:
Gen 15:1-6, 21:1-3; Col 3:12-17; Lk 2:22-40

Gift of Gratitude

I had the great pleasure of spending the last few days with my brother and his family in Sacramento. It is amazing how quickly their children grow up and how their new maturity comes out in subtle ways. It is very interesting to see how they receive and unwrap gifts. Daniella, my niece, is 5 years old and when she received a gift, she opened it excitedly and then thanked whoever gave it to her with a hug. 'Thank you, Uncle Brendan.' She did this with every gift.

Dominic, my nephew, who is only 3 years old, when he received a gift, he ripped it open, played with it for a second and then opened the next gift. When all the gifts were open he demanded to have the one gift he did not have. 'I want that!' he said pointing to his sister's new Barbie doll horse. 'No, you want to have the Spiderman toy!' I said. But he insisted all the more. 'I want that!' pointing again. So Daniella, without much bother, let him play with it all night as she continued to play with her other new toys.

What a difference a few years can make! I think sometimes we can act like my three-year-old nephew. We see other people's gifts and we want them without recognising or exploring the gifts we already have. I do not mean Christmas gifts, although that might be true too. I mean our natural, God-given gifts.

We often say, I want to be able to sing like that. Or I want to be able to play music like that. Or I want to be a sportsperson like that. Or I want to be good-looking like that. Or I want to be rich and famous like that. I want that!

In today's readings we hear, in the letter to the Colossians, a list of attributes we are encouraged to have as Christians: to put on kindness, gentleness, and patience and above all put on love. 'And whatever you do, in word or in deed, do everything in the name of the Lord Jesus, giving thanks to God the Father through him.' We are called to give God thanks for what we already have. At Christmas we tend to look at what others have and want that. Instead we are called to look at all we have and be thankful.

In whatever we do or say we are called to give thanks to God.
That is part of being a good steward. In the gospel today we hear
how Joseph and Mary offered thanks to God for the gift of their
son, Jesus. This temple ritual was not a rudimentary task. This
was the essence of their faith as Jews – that God had gifted them
with a child, and they responded by offering back their son in
thanksgiving. It was custom to offer in sacrifice the child at the
altar of the Lord but substitute the turtle doves or pigeons *in lieu*
of the child. The pagans around them often offered their
youngest child as a sacrifice to appease the gods, killing one of
their children. But in Judaism they offered animals in replace-
ment of the human sacrifice.

So Joseph and Mary were not only honouring their tradition
but they were truly thankful to God for the gift of their son. They
blessed the Lord for the gift and offered their son back in thanksgiving.

As we celebrate the Feast of the Holy Family, we honour our
tradition of the family as a sacred space. We recognise the gift
that we all have in our families, not that they are perfect places
but sacred spaces where holiness grows, and offer thanks to
God. One of the ways holiness grows is through the gift of gratitude – being grateful to God for all he has already given.

And so we come to this table of sacrifice today and say to the
Lord, we are grateful for everything he has given us. We offer
ourselves at this table and promise to be thankful.

This week and indeed this year ahead may we be grateful
and may we teach our children the gift of gratitude.
And whatever we do, in word or in deed,
do everything in the name of the Lord Jesus,
giving thanks to God the Father through him.

Mary, Mother of God
Num 6:22-27; Gal 4:4-7; Lk 2:16-21

I say 'Yes, my Lord'

There is the story told about Young Kathleen who was so excited about her part in the Christmas pageant. Her parents and family were all there, and one by one the children took their places. Mary and Joseph, played by two of the oldest, stood solemnly behind the manger. In the back, three young Wise Men waited impatiently. At the edge of the stage, Kathleen sat quietly and confidently. Then the teacher began: 'A long time ago, Mary and Joseph had a baby and they named him Jesus.' She continued, 'And when Jesus was born, a bright star appeared over the stable.' At that cue, Kathleen got up, picked up a large tinfoil star, walked behind Mary and Joseph and held the star up high for everyone to see.

When the teacher told about the shepherds coming to see the baby, the three young shepherds came forward, and Kathleen jiggled the star up and down excitedly to show them where to come.

When the Wise Men responded to their cue, Kathleen went forward a little to meet them and to lead the way. Her face was as brilliant as the original star must have been.

The little play ended, followed by refreshments. On the way home Kathleen said to her parents with great satisfaction, 'I had the main part.' 'You did?' her father questioned, wondering why she thought that. 'Yes,' she said, 'because I showed everybody how to find Jesus.'

How true! To show others how to find Jesus, to be the light for their paths in their lives – that is the finest role we can play in life.[1]

This is the role that Mary played all her life, she has always pointed to Christ. Today we celebrate the Solemnity of Mary, Mother of God, and we look to her life for wisdom for our lives. We look to her because she was human, but blessed in a special way.

In Mary, God has realised first and perfectly his design for the whole church and for each individual Christian. In other words, who Mary is, we are destined to be. So when we talk about Mary, we are talking about ourselves. We are proclaiming the ideal for a Christian.

'She is the perfect Christian, for she is perfectly redeemed. In her life and person she expresses to perfection what it means to believe, to love and to be loved, to be graced, to be saved.'[2] In her, we see in living flesh the meaning of redemption and true Christian purity.

In all she did and said, she pointed to Christ. She is the perfect imitation of Jesus and gives us a way to be the light of the world and a new way of being. She most exemplified this in her response to the angel's request by saying 'Let it be done onto me as you say.' She then conceived Jesus within her womb.

She said 'Yes, my Lord.'

I believe we too can conceive the Christ within us, by simply responding 'Yes, my Lord' to each request from our God to be part of our lives.

But we must listen as Mary listened; we must be prepared to make the difficult choices, to say 'Yes' when we know the choice will not be popular with those around us.

So today maybe we can listen more carefully to God's call to us and imitate Mary's perfect example and say 'Yes, my Lord.'

1. Brian Cavanagh, *Sower's Seeds Aplenty* (New Jersey: Paulist Press, 1996) #74.
2. Walter J. Burghardt SJ, *Tell the Next Generation*, (New Jersey: Paulist Press, 1980) 199.

God climbs in with us!

'The Word was made flesh and dwelt among us.'

There is a story told about a grandmother who found her grandson crying at the top of his voice, jumping up and down in his playpen.When Johnnie saw his grandmother, he reached up with his little chubby hands and said, 'Out, grandma, out.' It was only natural for the grandmother to reach down to lift him out of his predicament. But as she did, Johnnie's mother stepped up and said, 'No, Johnnie, you are being punished – so you must stay in.'

The grandmother was at a loss to know what to do. Johnnie's tears and chubby hands reached deep into her heart. But the mother's firmness in correcting her son must not be taken lightly.

Yet, love found a way! The grandmother could not take the grandson out of the playpen, so she climbed into the playpen with him.[1]

That is what our loving Father in heaven did for us, when he sent his only Son to become human in Jesus Christ. 'The Word became flesh and dwelt among us.' In leaving heaven for earth, he climbed in with us; he became one of us through the miracle and mystery of the incarnation.

From the beginning of our history as a people of God, we are assured of God's presence, that God is with us. When God forged a covenant with Abraham, renewed again with Isaac and Moses, and with all the prophets, the message was the same, 'I am with you.'

But we, as a people, got lost, and so he became one of us to show us the way back to God. Jesus Christ became one of us to show us the way, the way in this world, the way through this world and the way beyond this world.

Through Christ, God is with us in every way, in every human experience, in every adventure we take, in every sorrow we endure.

This new way is the way of love. So then, the question is how do we find this new way or remain in this way of life with Christ? God guides us from within ourselves, through his voice that we often call our conscience. We can come to understand his way for us, if we can only learn to listen.

Most of us have experienced some time of crisis and the feeling of not knowing what to do. Then suddenly, the way forward becomes clear – that voice within us guides us. Listening to this voice is not always easy. One consistent message God gives us in our heart is that we ought to love each other as he loved us. That is the summary of his way. Simple, but not easy!

This week may we take the time to listen to the inner voice trying to guide us back to God. Then may we act on that advice and find a new way to love others. There is always someone who needs our love. Whoever it is, may we love someone today and proclaim by action that 'The Word was made flesh and now dwells among us.'

1. James S. Hewett, *Illustrations Unlimited*, (Wheaton, Illinois: Tyndale House Publishers, 1988) 301.

Open our Eyes and See the Light of Christ

After Christmas this year I had the opportunity to visit and ski with my brother in Utah. One of the things I love most about going to the mountains is the cold and clear nights. It seems that the evening skies are so much darker in the mountains. And those stars seem so much brighter! The skies are studded with so many stars.

In moments like that, it is hard not to believe in God's love. It feels like God is there in the vastness of the sky. We are not alone. God is showering us with the brightness of his love.

Have you ever been in the mountains and seen those bright stars at night?

In our gospel reading today, the same feeling must have been felt by the magi as they discovered the true light. They saw the star which served as their guide in finding the Messiah. They believed that the heavenly wonder symbolised the birth of a heavenly person. For them, the bright guiding star was a sign. It was the symbol of the Christ.

Today we celebrate the feast of the Epiphany, which means a festival of light, the manifestation of the light of Jesus Christ in the darkness of the world. It is the celebration and the affirmation that we are not left out in the dark. Isaiah reminds us of that symbolism when he says: 'Arise, shine, for the glory of the Lord has risen upon you.' (Is 60:1)

It is only in finding the star – like the magi in our gospel – and following its divine path that we can be brought to the true joy and happiness in God. Remember that after seeing the Messiah and offering their gifts of gold, frankincense, and myrrh, the magi changed their path, and that symbolises conversion, a transformation in their lives.

In our lives as well, we too have the star or light in our own hearts and we are called to change our path and follow Christ. Each of us has gifts and those are the mark of our creator. We have the bright light of Christ burning within our hearts. Yet there are times we don't believe that truth. We sometimes fail to recognise his presence in ourselves and in others.

In this age of electricity and artificial lights, it is difficult to appreciate the symbolism of light. However, it is still a powerful image to use in describing life's difficulties and joys. When we experience the loss of property, material wealth, our health, or even a loved one, we feel that we are in the dark without hope. We even have an expression when we do not know about something. We say, 'We are in the dark.'

Now, I want to try another experiment. I want all of you to close your eyes. No! This time you will not be pregnant and you will not use your imagination. Just close your eyes and feel the darkness you see. Peer into the depths of that darkness. Experience it for a second. Okay, open your eyes.

Feel the rush of light in your eyes. That is how it is with Jesus. In Christ, God gave us the light of the world. He continues to give us the light through signs, which we have in our heart. But if we are too busy with our selfish desires and other matters, then we will not notice the light of the star. It is only when we look up away from our selfish desires and our preoccupations that we can notice it.

If only we can open our eyes to the light of Christ within us and within others then we will find our path in life. This week, we are also celebrating National Vocation Awareness Week, and we are encouraged to seek the will of God for us, that light within us that guides us and others back to God. We ask ourselves this week, and especially today on this the feast of the Epiphany, what is the best gift we can offer to the Messiah? Could it be our time, maybe just an hour to be with Jesus in the Mass, a couple of hours more spent with our loved ones, maybe a moment with a friend or neighbour?

Before we can bring the light of Christ to others, we must first recognise the light of Christ within us. We ought to open our eyes and see that bright star shining in us. So as we take down the lights of our Christmas trees and the lights outside on our houses, maybe we can be reminded that we keep the light of Christ burning within us.

The Baptism of the Lord:
Is 55:1-11; 1 Jn 5:1-9; Mk 1:7-11

Come with an Appetite!

Over the Christmas holidays I got invited to a lot of parties. I am sure that many of you had the same issue. Well one night I accepted offers to go to visit three different parties. I had planned to go to the first house to eat only appetisers. Then to the second house and eat the main course. Then finally to the last house for dessert. That was the plan!

I got to the first house and I could not get out of there until I had 'sampled' everything. When I went to the second place I was full, but I managed to eat another full meal. Eventually I made it to the third place but I was truly stuffed. Of course, a full meal awaited me. I tried but could not eat anything more ... I was too full.

Obviously my friends were not happy that I was not going to eat with them. The irony of the story was that I tried to please all three families and I suspect that instead I insulted all three families. After all, when we invite someone for dinner we expect him or her to come with an appetite to eat.[1] It is rude to do otherwise.

When we come to the table of the Lord every Sunday at his invitation, the Lord expects us to have an appetite. But sometimes, or even most times, we come without an appetite. We come to the table out some sort of habit ... not that habit is bad ... it is good to be here. But there is more than just coming here out of habit.

We are expected to have an appetite for his food for our souls. We are expected to be ready to listen attentively to scripture and be fed with the words of life. Yes, we are expected to come with an appetite for his food.

Today we celebrate the baptism of the Lord and we are reminded of our own baptism. We are reminded of the day we were first invited to the Lord's Table. We are reminded of the first day we said 'yes' or someone said it for us. We were washed clean and offered nourishment for the journey. Every Sunday since, we have been invited to his table for more food.

Jesus' baptism was different than ours insofar as we are forgiven our sins, while he took onto himself all the sins of the world. His baptism was not only water but blood and the Spirit.

31

He gave us his own Spirit and promised to feed us always with his own body and blood. So each Sunday we are expected to come with an appetite.

When the water of baptism was poured over us once, back a long time ago, it was a special day. It happened once but we are called to renew every week. Some say it is the most important day of our lives. Even more important than our First Communion or Confirmation or Marriage or Ordination to priesthood days because we have been invited to the table of the Lord. But every week is important because we get an opportunity to renew ourselves with the food from the table. But we must come with an appetite.

We can create an appetite for this table by dusting off our bibles and taking small bites in reading it daily. Yes, open your bible and see what the Lord is saying directly to you. Open up your day from the busyness of life and give him some time. Get to know Jesus a little better with devoting some time to prayer. I mean find a space where you can be with the Lord for a few minutes. Read scripture for a few minutes each day and listen to what he has to say. Then when we come here to this table we are ready, with our hearts hungry for what the Lord has to say to us. We will hear scripture as if it was being spoken to us directly. We will eat and drink the bread and wine, knowing that it is nourishment for our souls.

Yes, he will feed us at this banquet if we come with an appetite.

1. Inspired by *Homily Helps*, (St Anthony Messenger Press: Cincinnati, OH, January, 2003).

Fast and Feast

Return to me with your whole heart, with fasting, and weeping, and
mourning. Rend your hearts and not your garments, and return to the
Lord, your God. (Joel 2:13)

About ninety years ago a man picked up the morning paper
and, to his horror, read his own obituary! The newspaper had
reported the death of the wrong man. Like most of us, he rel-
ished the idea of finding out what people would say about him
after he died. He read past the bold caption that read, 'Dynamite
King Dies', to the text itself. He read along until he was taken
back by the description of him as a 'merchant of death'.

He was the inventor of dynamite and amassed a great for-
tune from the manufacture of weapons of destruction. But he
was moved by this description. Did he really want to be known
as a 'merchant of death'? A healing power greater than the destructive force of the dynamite came over him. It was his hour of
conversion. From that point on, he devoted his energy and
money to works of peace and justice. He worked for the building up and not the tearing down, of the human community.

Today, of course, he is best remembered, not as a 'merchant
of death', but as the founder of the Nobel Peace Prize – Alfred
Nobel.[1]

How would our obituary read today? Would people say that
we tear down the community or build it up? When we look at
our lives, like Alfred Nobel, do we see some bad habits or actions that need changing?

Well today starts another season of Lent and the gospel urges
us to be on our guard against religious acts for people to see. In
other words, the gospel urges us to be authentic in our actions.
We are called to pray in secret and fast so nobody knows we are
fasting. So how do we accomplish these tasks?

I suggest we need to start with an honest look at ourselves,
like Alfred Nobel in the story. Are all my actions in continuity
with the gospel? What behaviour needs changing today? How
do I open myself to the ongoing process of conversion of my
own heart?

Fortunately, we are given 40 days for contemplation of our

behaviour and the task to change it. And if we are honest, I think we will need all 40 days.

Yet it really is a joy-filled season because in turning back toward God we realise that he welcomes us with open arms and will never leave us. He gives us the very courage to turn back to him and the strength to walk toward him. What a wonderful gift to accept!

In a few moments the ashes will be distributed and while making a cross on our foreheads the words 'Turn away from sin and be faithful to the gospel' are said.

Let me suggest this Lenten season that instead of giving something up in penance we fast from a sin and feast on a gospel value! For example, if we fast from hatred, and feast on love. Fast from pride and feast on humility. Fast from selfishness and feast on service.

I suggest that we take 20 minutes today and make up our own short list of sins we will fast from and gospel values we will feast on instead. In this way the Lenten journey to Easter will be a true journey into our own hearts.[2]

Return to me with your whole heart, with fasting, and weeping, and mourning. Rend your hearts and not your garments, and return to the Lord, your God. (Joel 2:13)

1. Brian Cavanaugh, *The Sower's Seeds*, (Mahwah, New Jersey: Paulist Press, 1990) #54.
2. Other sources: Carroll Stuhlmueller, CP, *Biblical Meditations For Lent*, (Mahwah, New Jersey: Paulist Press, 1980), Megan McKenna, *Lent: The Daily Readings*, (Maryknoll, New York: Orbis Books, 1997) 2-6, *The Word Among Us*, Lent (1999).

First Sunday of Lent:
Deut 26:4-10; Rom 10:8-13; Lk 4:1-13

Time-Out! Leave the Baggage behind!

Last Tuesday I had the opportunity to watch the Boys Basketball Varsity Team of St Lawrence High School Academy[1] play in the semi-final of the championship. It was the first time in the history of the school that we made it to the semi-finals and a very exciting moment for our parish. It was a great game with many exciting moments. But at several times throughout the game, especially in the last moments of it, the coach called time-outs. The time-out helped the coach re-focus the team's efforts and almost always they scored immediately afterwards. In the last quarter, with seconds to go, they took a time-out and scored 8 points in just 3 plays. The time-outs were very important to the success of the game.

You parents are familiar with the same concept when your children are acting up. We say, 'No, go to your room right now,' or 'Stop that right now or you will get a time-out.' It is an effective means of discipline for unruly kids. It is our effort to get the children to stop what they are doing or to reconsider their current actions.

Well the church has a time-out and it is called Lent.[2] It is the time that the church calls us to stop what we are currently doing and examine our lives to see if we ought to continue these actions. It is the time that we re-focus our lives on the important things. After many years of Lents we are probably all familiar with the three ways in which the church asks us to journey: prayer, fasting, and alms giving. These are the three wheels upon which we journey together to Easter.

Well, in today's gospel we hear Jesus take a time-out, spend some time alone with God in prayer, fast from food, and examine his life. Then he came from the desert and gave alms in the greatest way – he gave of himself. We are called to follow his example. So how do we go about doing this?

There are many ways but let me suggest one we can do together. It is best illustrated by a story: There was a woman who moved houses recently and hired some professional movers to pack for her. When the movers arrived they asked what she wanted packed. With some satisfaction she said, 'Take it all', waving her arms around the place. When she arrived at her new house she realised that the movers had taken her quite literally. Along with the furniture they had packed up her trash bins too. There she was in her new place with all her old garbage including newspapers, empty ketchup bottles and even some old orange peels she had left on the counter top.[3]

I think when we move from one place to another in our lives we often take our garbage with us. When we move from one season to another, or one year to another, we take things with us we really don't need. As we switch seasons there is a temptation to do the same.

In this season of Lent maybe we do not need to take everything with us. Maybe we can rid ourselves of some garbage this Lent. Maybe we can take a time-out and examine what are some of the things each of us can leave behind. What are some of the things we can fast from? Maybe we have been hurt recently or a long time ago and we do not need to take that baggage with us. Is it time to let it go? Fast from the anger. Maybe there is some other anger we need to fast from. We are invited to examine our lives and see what garbage we need to fast from.

Or maybe we can give alms, giving from our very selves like Jesus did. Alms giving is more than giving money – it's about giving from ourselves. Maybe we can volunteer for our community or spend some more time with family or friends genuinely listening to their concerns or fears.

Whatever it is this week, we can take a time-out and spend some time with God, praying and examining our lives, finding something to fast from and somehow to give of our very selves. This week we can change ourselves on this Lenten journey by taking a time-out and leaving some baggage behind.

1. This is the Secondary School belonging to the parish at which I serve.
2. Adapted from *Celebration: An Ecumenical Worship Resource*, (Kansas City, MO: National Catholic Reporter Company, Inc., March, 2001).
3. Adapted from William J. Bausch, *Story Telling the Word*, (Mystic, Connecticut: Twenty-Third Publications, 1996) 168.

Second Sunday of Lent:
Gen 15:5-12, 17-18; Phil 3:17-4:1; Lk 9:28-36

Transfigured into Christ

In Ireland we love to talk about the weather. Nearly all of our greetings have some comment on the weather. For example on a sunny day with blue skies a person might say, 'Tis a grand day now. Although look at those clouds, there might be rain yet!' Or on a rainy gloomy day someone might say, 'Tis is a soft day now but I think the clouds are breaking up, and isn't that the sun peeking from behind the clouds?' We seem to recognise the natural cycle in the weather: the sun always follows the rain and sooner or later the rain follows the sun. In Ireland it always seems to be sooner rather than later!

I think this natural cycle mirrors what happens in our lives. I mean we have these experiences in our lives, that the sun is shining bright and clouds seem to be very far away. Things are going great and it is like we are on top of a mountain. It's an awesome experience. Maybe it is when we fall in love, those early days of love when we seem to float along. Or the time we hold our newborn child or grandchild; or finishing a big project we have laboured months on at work; entering our first new home or apartment, etc. The feeling is eternal. There seem to be no clouds.

Then there are those dark experiences where the clouds are evident. It is like a desert experience, often unwelcome and unwanted. Maybe it is the loss of a job or house. Or maybe a friend moves out of town or to another school. Or maybe it is some form of sickness and days seem to very long indeed. Or maybe it is the loss of a loved one. The desert seems to last forever. The rain seems to never end.

Yet we are people of the gospel, people of hope that the sun will shine again. Yes, there is a natural cycle to it all. Well, in last week's gospel we heard Jesus enter into his desert experience to be tempted by the devil after 40 days. And today we hear that on top of the mountain Jesus reveals himself to his disciples in all his glory. Christ reveals himself in all his brilliance and shows who he really is – the Son of God!

Yet these two sections are not contiguous in the gospel, they are chapters apart. So why does the church put them in this order for us to read? One reason is that the church is trying to bolster our faith. In Lent we are called to a radical conversion of our own hearts and, in case we lose heart in this endeavour after we enter the desert experience, the church wants us to keep sight of God's presence in our lives.[1] It encourages us to not give up in our struggles but to believe in that ray of sunshine that hides behind the cloud. It encourages us to persevere in our conversion.

So how do we hear this message today? In the twenty-first century how can this affect us?

Let me suggest that we can look at the week that has just gone and ask whether I saw something or experienced something that revealed the presence of Christ. Maybe it was the kiss of a loved one or maybe the loving hug or touch of our parent or child. Maybe it was a kind comment made that made our week. Or maybe we saw someone do something profound this week. Yes, we ought to reflect to see where I experienced Christ this week. Then we can also ask, how can I reveal Christ to others this week? I mean, is there something I can do that would make someone else's week? Maybe it is that loving kiss, hug, or touch.

Or maybe it is writing a card or letter to someone who we care about but have taken for granted so often. Maybe it is getting in touch with someone who we have lost touch with.

Is it forgiving an old grudge? Or is it listening to someone desperately needing a call?

This week maybe we can reveal Christ to others by allowing the grace of God to work in and through us. Maybe we can take the radical conversion of our hearts seriously by saying or doing something that reveals God's love to others and so be transfigured ourselves into Christ.

---

1. Inspired by comments from Robert Waznak, SS, *Like Fresh Bread*, (Mahwah, New Jersey: Paulist Press, 1993) 48.

Third Sunday of Lent:
Ex 3:1-8, 13-15; 1 Cor 10:1-6, 10-12; Lk 13:1-9

Second Chance!

Several years ago, when I was working as an executive in the high-tech world, my staff had a problem with the way I was managing the office. One day they went to my boss, the Chairman of the Board, and gave him a laundry list of complaints about me. Then my boss met with me to go over the list. It was a long list!

It was very humbling if not humiliating to be confronted with every flaw I had. It made it even more difficult that it was coming from someone other than the people who had the problem. However, I took a week off work to examine their issues and to pray significantly about it.

In prayer, I realised that most of the problems centred around the same issue – they felt I did not listen to them. So I went back to work after about a week and sat with them as a group. I asked them to forgive me and give me a second chance. They agreed eagerly and we put together a specific action plan.

That day and that week changed the office environment forever. We were all more honest and more communicative. The office environment became one of mutual support. It was the day I learned a valuable lesson: the willingness of others to give me a second chance and the need to ask for a second chance.

Have you ever been forgiven and been given a second chance? Maybe it was your parent or child over something small. Or maybe it was your spouse over something big. Or maybe it was a friend or co-worker. Whether over something big or small, I think we have all received a second chance sometime in our life, a chance to start over.

In today's gospel Jesus tells the parable of the fig tree in response to questions about apparent injustices. Jesus reminds his listeners that we ought not to judge. We were all given a second chance even though we do not produce much fruit. Jesus calls all of us to give others a second chance as we were given a second chance by God.

As we continue our Lenten journey and reflect on our lives maybe we can ask ourselves who in our lives is in need of a second chance from us. Who is desperately waiting another chance to start over? Is there someone whom we can forgive and give a new lease on life to? Maybe it is our child because of something they have recently done. Or maybe it is our parent for forgetting their grandchild's birthday. Or maybe it is a friend who betrayed us or someone at work with whom we do not see eye to eye. Or maybe we are the one in need of a second chance.

Can we ask someone for another chance? Maybe it is our parent or child we need forgiveness from. Or maybe it is our spouse because of some serious problem. Or maybe we need to go to someone at work and ask for a second chance.

Whether we are the ones in need of a second chance or the ones who can offer a second chance, this week we can take the Lenten journey a little more seriously together. We can each ask ourselves who in our life needs a second chance and who do I need a second chance from. Then we can offer thanks and praise next Sunday for a second chance at living the gospel anew this week. This week give someone a second chance![1]

---

1. Sources used but not quoted explicitly: *Celebration: An Ecumenical Worship Resource*, (Kansas City, MO: National Catholic Reporter Company, Inc., March, 2001), Jude Siciliano, OP, *Preachers Exchange*, (Raleigh, NC: preachex@opsouth.org).

Fourth Sunday of Lent:
Josh 5:9-12; 2 Cor 5:17-21; Lk 15:1-3, 11-32

Spring Cleaning Our Lives!

As many of you know, I try to walk every morning around the neighbourhood. Recently, I have noticed the neighbourhood has changed. Have you noticed? I mean it is a mess! Everyone has major amounts of trash outside their houses. Well, after some investigation, I found out it is spring cleaning for the entire city of Santa Clara. We all can put our garbage, as much as we want, on the sidewalks and the city collects it for *free*. Wow! I have never seen nor heard of such a thing before. It is a great idea, isn't it? Everybody works on their little patch and cleans it up. Then the city supplies the garbage collectors and it's all done. Everybody does spring cleaning together.

Well the church supplies a time for spiritual spring cleaning and it is called Lent. This is the time we communally clean our little patches and put our spiritual garbage on our spiritual sidewalks so God can collect it and dispense with it. We can put all our little sins or large ones on the sidewalks of our lives.

Lent after all actually means spring and it is that time of year we reflect on our lives and see where we need a conversion of our own hearts. In a special way we will do this together when we gather for the communal reconciliation on two weeks from Tuesday. In this communal act of reconciliation we all work on our little patches and take our spiritual garbage to the sidewalk of our spiritual lives. In the same way when we plan to clean our houses we also must clean our spiritual lives by admitting our sins and asking for forgiveness.

In today's gospel we hear one of the most profound examples of reconciliation in the bible – the story of the prodigal son. What parent in his/her right mind would forgive so easily the greedy young son of today's story? He asks for half of his father's estate and then squanders it only to return for forgiveness. What a powerful example of forgiveness!

Not only does God want to forgive us our sins but he rejoices at the fact we return to him. Like the younger brother we want to go humbly before God and ask for forgiveness for all our sins, even the big ones. At that sight God not only forgives but celebrates our willingness to be reconciled.

In the second reading, to the Corinthians, we are reminded that God wants us to be reconciled with him and we are called to be ambassadors for Christ. We are invited to be reconciled with God and with one another. We ought not to be like the older brother who begrudges his father's forgiveness to his younger brother. We ought not to look at our neighbour's garbage and complain that they are littering our neighbourhood. Instead, like the father, we ought to celebrate their willingness to clean house and ask for forgiveness.

So this week we are called to look at our own lives and ask where in my life do I need to seek forgiveness, where in my life I need reconciliation. Maybe it is our parents who we seem to argue with endlessly; maybe it is because they never remember the grand children's (your children's) birthdays. Or maybe it is our children because we never see them anymore. Maybe it is a friend whom you argued with and never reconciled. Or maybe it is your spouse over some domestic issue. Whatever it is, this week we are called to examine our lives and seek reconciliation with God our Father and with one another.

This week maybe we can spring clean our spiritual lives and prepare for the communal spiritual spring cleaning at the Rite of Communal Reconciliation. This week maybe we can spring clean just a little in preparation for Easter.

Fifth Sunday of Lent:
Is 43:16-21; Phil 3:8-14; Jn 8:1-11

Put Down Our Stones and Forgive

Several years a friend of mine was telling me about her attending traffic school. She had two speeding tickets and she did not want a third on her licence. When she attended the traffic school the officer asked the group a question: 'How many of you think you did not deserve this ticket?' About 85% of the hands went up. Then the officer asked, 'How many of you have never, ever, ever broken the speed limit?' This time no hands went up. The officer then explained that while this occasion you might or might not have deserved the ticket, the reality is that you have broken the law lots of times and only now have been caught.

In the same way each and every one of us has sinned at some time. If we are honest with ourselves we will admit that we can sin quite regularly in small ways. However, most times our sins are not known to others but known only to us and God. Indeed often we do not even see our own sins. But when we reflect on our lives we realise how far short we have fallen from our goal of the Christian life.

In today's gospel we hear about a woman who was caught in the act of committing adultery. She was caught and the Pharisees wanted to stone her for that sin because the law said they could do so. They brought her to Jesus not only to punish the woman but also to test Jesus. The woman is also being used by the Pharisees and scribes. Yet Jesus sees through their rather shallow efforts and tells them, 'he who is without sin throw the first stone.' The elders are the first to leave because they realise that they are definitely *not* without sin. And soon all the others follow their lead. No one could throw a stone because no one is without sin. Then Jesus tells her that he will not condemn her either and tells her to sin no more.

Isn't that what we ought to do for one another – realise that we are *not* without sin and *not* throw stones at others whose sins are known. We are called not to judge others. Jesus tells us not to judge for we will be judged.

However, every day we are called to make judgements so how could this be? We have to make judgements between right and wrong, between the merits of one thing and another constantly. Will I go here or there? Will I do my homework or watch TV? Will I work hard or be lazy? Will I speed or not? etc. But this is not the 'judgement' that Jesus was referring to. The Greek and Hebrew word that is translated 'judge' is more accurately defined as 'condemn'. Actually the words are often switched in different translations and indeed are used interchangeably. For example, 'Do not judge and you will not be condemned.' (Lk 6:37) So Jesus is saying that we are not to condemn and specifically today he is saying to us we ought not to condemn others who sin because we are all sinners.

Yes, we are called to judge in the sense of evaluate each day but we are called not to judge others in the sense of condemning others. We are all called to put down our stones and forgive. Forgive as our Father has forgiven us.

So as we leave here today maybe we can ask ourselves who have I judged or condemned? Is there a family member we have cast aside in judgement because of some long ago action? Is there a friend who is no longer 'friend' because we have condemned his or her actions? Is there someone in our lives whom we need to not only *not* condemn but also forgive as our Father has forgiven us? This week maybe we can put our stones of judgement down and forgive.

Following Christ through Apparent Failure

In business there is a wise adage that says, 'We are defined by our failures.' Well today we hear, in the passion of our Lord Jesus Christ, possibly the greatest failure in history. Here is the Son of God and he dies on a cross.

Or is it a failure? Yes, on the outside it appears to be failure, but we believe and know that it is not a failure, but the greatest triumph in all of history. Jesus Christ overcomes even death. He turns failure into success.

However, there is more to it than that. How he handles his apparent failure is equally as important as the fact that he apparently fails. So to put that old adage differently, 'How we handle our failures is how we will be remembered.' Indeed a boss of mine once said to me, 'Brendan, *how* you fail, not *if* you fail, will be your evaluation in this job.' Maybe a little intimidating, but realistic! I believe that it is a fact of life that we will fail at things, both personally and professionally. Some say if we don't fail, we are not trying hard enough. To live is to fail or suffer in some way, especially with our health. So the question becomes *how well* do we suffer or fail? And where do we turn?

We can turn to Jesus for a fine example of how to suffer well and how to live with pain or apparent failure. Looking at today's scripture alone we hear how Jesus heals even while he is being arrested. When his disciples draw a sword on the guard and cut off his ear Jesus immediately heals the man. Then on the cross itself the thieves are mocking him and he turns to one thief and offers him forgiveness. Jesus ministers right to the last moment. He never gives up. He does not stop doing what he was called to do because of some apparent failure. He never gives up doing the Father's will – he heals, forgives, and preaches to his last breath.

What shall we be like when we face failure or suffering? If we wait until the moment of pain's arrival, then we will only have time to react (without thought). No, we ought to decide *now*, so that we will do the Father's will right to our last breath. Today and this week may we decide and promise that when we face suffering or failure we will turn to God the Father. We will iden-

tify with Christ in all his suffering, continuing to do his will right
to our last breath.

Bend Low and Serve

In today's first reading from the Book of Exodus we hear how the Lord told the people of Israel to celebrate the Passover by taking a one-year-old lamb and slaughtering it on the altar of the Lord. Then take and eat its flesh that same night to celebrate. That was, and is, the Jewish custom to remember how the Lord saved his people from the Egyptians.

Then along comes Jesus who says that we do not need to sacrifice a lamb any longer because he is the Lamb of God. He is the one who will take away the sins of the world. He says that he sacrifices himself on this altar of the cross. We no longer need to offer any animal sacrifices but offer our own lives in service to others.

We are called to remember his last meal in which he took the bread and said 'Take and eat', then took the wine and said 'Take and drink.' Do this in memory of him.

Do you ever wonder what the 'this' is? To be sure it is this eucharistic celebration of the Mass we celebrate today, every day and every Sunday, but I believe it is more. We are called to come to this table and offer ourselves at this table along with his one sacrifice. We are invited to offer ourselves to one another. We are invited to become bread for others. We are called to become what we receive, the bread for the world, broken and shared for all to have. We are called to love one another as Jesus taught us. That is the 'this' I believe – to love one another as Jesus has loved us.

Then Jesus showed us a working example of this love. He turned around at the table and washed the disciples' feet. A job for the lowliest servant to do. It was the job of a slave and if the house had no slave then it was the youngest member of the household. Jesus turned everything upside down. He wanted us to understand as disciples that we are called to serve one another. That means we are called to serve all, not just our friends and family. We are called most especially to serve those we do not like. The washing of feet is a reminder to us that we need to bend low and serve others, especially when times are tough.

This last week has not been an easy week for us Catholics. In particular it has not been an easy week for us priests. Every day we have read in the headlines of the scandal within the church. But all the more we are now called to bend even lower in service to one another remembering that it was the one eternal sacrifice of Christ Jesus that saves us all. He set the example.

Yes, in the midst of all this we are called to bend lower now in service, to serve and support one another. Who is it we need to bend low to and serve? It may not even be someone we like but it is someone close by. We are called to bend low and serve.

Easter Sunday: Day Mass:
Acts 10:34, 37-43; Col 3:1-4; Jn 20:1-9

Moving Beyond the Cross

Every year thousands of people go on pilgrimage climbing a mountain in the Italian Alps, passing the 'stations of the cross' to stand at a large wooden crucifix depicting the crucifixion of Christ Jesus. One year, a pilgrim noticed a little trail that led beyond the cross. She fought through the overgrown and unused trail, and to her surprise, came upon another shrine, a shrine that symbolised the empty tomb. It was neglected. The brush had grown up around it. Almost everyone had gone as far as the cross, but there they stopped.

So many of us experience the cross in our lives. So many of us know despair and heartbreak in our lives. Maybe it is the loss of a job at work or maybe trouble with friends at school or work; maybe it is a break or fracture in the family. Or maybe it is the death of a loved one. Whatever pain we have in our lives it seems at times to overwhelm us.

We often ask, where is God now? Where is my God now in my hour of need? It seems so hard to believe in the midst of all the pain. It is sometimes hard to move beyond the cross.

But remember the full story. There is something beyond the cross. There is more to Christ than the cross. There is the empty tomb.

So there is hope beyond the pain and despair of our lives. The empty tomb symbolises that hope because it points to the resurrection of Christ Jesus. Christ Jesus is alive! Alive in us.[1]

In today's gospel we hear how the disciples come to the empty tomb and, upon seeing it empty, they believe Christ is risen. They do not understand exactly what has happened, but they believe.

This experience of the disciples is mirrored in our lives too. When we are in the midst of pain and despair we are called to believe even though we do not understand. We are called to believe that Christ is always there by our side. We are called to move beyond the cross. The empty tomb is the symbol and reality of the Risen Christ. This is a cornerstone of our faith as Christians.

Without the resurrection, Christianity would not exist. As

Paul says to the Corinthians, 'If Christ has not been raised, then empty is our preaching; empty is our faith.' (1 Cor 15:15) But where is he risen to? How does that help me get through the pain of life?

When we celebrate the eucharist at this table, we celebrate the Risen Christ and his presence here among us. We offer praise and thanks to God for all he has done, all he continues to do, and promises to do in the future. One of those promises is to be with us always. In a special way, here at eucharist we believe there are four presences of Christ – yes, we know that he is present in the species of bread and wine, but also in the community, the People of God, the proclaimed Word of God, and finally in the person of the priest. Yes, we offer praise and thanksgiving every week and indeed every day for the gift of his presence among us at this table.

Then the question becomes, how do we make his presence known to others around us? How do we let our faith, our belief inform our very actions?

Let me suggest that we become Christ to others. When we are there for someone in pain then we become the Risen Lord to them. We are their hope. We can be Christ to each other. When someone is in pain then we have an opportunity to be Christ to them. Maybe it is time to repair that broken relationship. To write that letter to our forgotten friend. To pick up the phone to that family member long estranged from the family.

Today may we be the Risen Christ to our brother, sister, friend or stranger. Today may we be their empty tomb, giving them hope beyond their cross.

1. Adapted from James S. Hewett, *Illustrations Unlimited*, (Wheaton, Illinois: Tyndale House Publishers, Inc., 1988) 164.

In The Midst of Turmoil!

Chirppie the parakeet bird never saw it coming. One second the bird was peacefully perched in his cage. The next he was sucked in, washed up and blown over. Chirppie's owner decided to clean his cage with a vacuum cleaner. She stuck the neck of the hose in the cage. Then the phone rang. She picked up the phone and barely said hello when 'SSOPP!' and Chirppie was sucked into the vacuum. Chirppie's owner gasped in shock, dropped the phone, turned off the vacuum cleaner and ripped open the bag. There was Chirppie – still alive but stunned and covered in dust. She grabbed him and quickly ran to the bathroom and turned on the tap and held Chirppie under the running water to wash off the dust. Realising that Chirppie was soaked and shivering, she reached for her hair dryer and blasted the little bird with hot air. Then she put Chirppie back in his cage. Poor Chirppie never knew what hit him. A few days after the trauma, the reporter who covered the story contacted the owner again to see how Chirppie was and she said, 'He doesn't chirp much anymore but he just sits and stares!' It is not hard to see why! Sucked in, washed out, and blown over … that's enough to steal the song from anyone.[1]

Often in our lives we have things happen to us that make us feel sucked in, washed out, or blown over. Maybe it is the loss of a job while having trouble with your family. Or maybe it is a failing marriage while one of your friends is very sick. Sometimes life has a way of stacking the deck against us.

Well, in today's gospel the disciples feel the same way. They feel sucked in, washed out, and blown over. Their friend Jesus who they had come to believe was the Messiah, the chosen one to fulfill the scriptures, was not only dead but he was hung on a cross in shame. They were shattered and totally ashamed. Then to make matters worse his body was supposedly stolen from the tomb. And anybody who was associated with Jesus was in danger. They were terrified and so they locked themselves in a room to hide. While holed up inside that locked room, the risen Christ appears to them and says, 'Peace be with you.' And then he commands them to go and proclaim the gospel.

In the midst of their turmoil, doubting and pain, he appears to them and invites them to believe and proclaim the gospel. Well, the Catholic Church is feeling the pain. We are all ashamed of what a few men did. We are angry about the turmoil and doubt whether the hierarchy hears our pain. This has been a difficult month for us Catholics, especially for us priests. We have been sucked in, washed out and certainly blown over. The pain seems endless. The press seems to insist on blowing over it again and again.

Yes, these are difficult times and we might be tempted to hide in a locked room, so to speak. That is where the Risen Christ will be for us, in the middle of the pain and turmoil. It is there that we will receive the Risen Lord – right in the middle of it. And he says to go and proclaim the gospel.

So how do we proclaim the gospel in times like this? I suggest that we proclaim it by our actions now more than ever. Yes, this broken and beautiful church will be better for this pain. We will be purified by it and rise again. But we have to believe that! In the midst of being sucked in, washed out and blown over, we need to be willing to proclaim the gospel.

We are called to live like the disciples, loving one another in the good and the bad times. Who can we reach out to and be the Risen Lord? Who in our lives needs to break out of their locked rooms? Who is in fear or doubt or turmoil that needs a loving touch? Maybe it is someone within the church. We are called to be men and women of action.

This week as we go forth from here maybe we can live by the words of St Francis who says, 'Preach the gospel always, and if necessary use words!'

---

1. Max Lucado "In the Eye of the Storm," as quoted in *Connections* (Mediaworks, Londonderry, NH: April, 2002) 2.

Third Sunday of Easter:
Acts 5:27-32, 40-41; Rev 5:11-14; Jn 21:1-19

Messenger of Forgiveness

I have been ordained for only three years. At my age I am considered a late vocation. One of the reasons I was a late vocation was every time I heard God calling me I would answer, 'Lord, I am not good enough to be a priest.' And he would answer me, 'I did not choose you because you were good but because I wanted *you*.' Nonetheless I would ignore him as best as I could. Then later, after God got to me again, I would answer 'I am not holy enough,' but he would answer, 'I did not choose you because you were holy but because I wanted *you*.'

Well, as you can see, I lost the argument and I am a priest today. It is not because I am good or holy, but because God wanted me to do this and I agreed. Do you ever feel that you are not good enough or holy enough for what God asks of you on the Christian journey? Do you ever feel that God must be calling others to lead holy lives rather than you? I believe it is a common feeling that we believe we are not good or holy enough!

We even have company with the saints and the apostles themselves. Remember Peter, who is arguably the primary example of discipleship, as he denied Jesus after Jesus' arrest. He denied Jesus not once but three times. After that he did not feel like following Jesus any more. I am sure he felt he was not good enough or holy enough.

However, Jesus did not give up on Peter, nor does he give up on us. He wants to forgive us as he forgave Peter. He wants us to follow him as Peter followed him. In today's gospel we hear Jesus asking Peter how much he loves him. Jesus asks him three times if he loves him – three times because Jesus wants to repair and restore Peter to his true self and wipes away his three denials.

After Jesus' appearance and breakfast with Peter, Peter becomes all that God asks of him. He becomes a true disciple of Jesus Christ and preaches the message with undying enthusiasm and joy. And we are called to do the same as Peter in our own vocation in life. Jesus commands his disciples to preach to all the corners of the earth and to gather in all peoples into the unity of his church.

This is told in today's gospel in the symbolic language that John the evangelist is famous for. You see, the mention of catching 153 fish seems random to us, but in Jesus' time that was the number of species of fish in totality, according to the zoologists of the time.[1] Thus 153 symbolises all the peoples of the world.

The fact the net never broke suggests that the church will be united in Christ. God does not choose us because we are good or holy, but because he wants us to be part of his church, the People of God. He wants us to try to be good and holy, but he always forgives us when we fail. Indeed he seeks us out to give us forgiveness in the same way he sought out Peter. So this week how can we be messengers of God's loving forgiveness, and in so doing spread the message of Christ to the whole world? Who can we seek out to offer our forgiveness?

We have been chosen not because we are better or more holy than others but we are called to be his messengers in this world. Indeed it is often through our weaknesses we are made strong Christians. Today we can spread his message by seeking out someone who needs our forgiveness.

---

1. *Celebration: An Ecumenical Worship Resource*, (Kansas City, Mo: National Catholic Reporter Company, Inc., April, 2001).

Fourth Sunday of Easter:
Acts 13:14, 43-52; Rev 7:9, 14-17; Jn 10:27-30

Hearing God's Voice and Acting on it

Each week on my day off I try to go and visit with my brother and his family in Sacramento. Every time I arrive my brother asks his children who they think has arrived before they see me. They attempt a few wild guesses and then I say a couple of words! Recognising my voice they come running, screaming at the top of their voices – 'Uncle Breeendaaaan'.

How nice it is to be recognised by our voice! There are people in all of our lives whom we recognise by voice alone. How often when we answer the phone, upon hearing just a few words, we know exactly who it is? Usually it is our mother, father, spouse, child, or best friend. Whoever, we know our closest family and friends by their voices.

Yes, the comforting sounds of a loving voice! We especially rely on it in times of need. Remember back to a time when you were saddened over some event in your life, then a call came from a loving family member or friend and how it comforted you.

It seems to me that the same can be said about our relationship with God. If he is close as to us as family or friend then we will recognise the sound of his voice and be comforted by it, especially in the difficult times. So how do we listen to the voice of God? Especially in times of violence like what has happened in the last week in Colorado.[1] How do we listen to God's voice in the midst of such horrible events?

In today's gospel we hear the story of the Good Shepherd and the power of the shepherd's voice. However, when the gospel of John was written most of the community for whom it was written were farmers and the story of the Good Shepherd and his sheep was a very powerful illustration. Today, however, most of our lives are identified not with sheep or shepherds but with computers, the internet, television, and cellular phones. Perhaps if Jesus were telling the story in Silicon Valley, instead of being the Good Shepherd he would be the head of the latest internet portal search engine and if you want answers we can go there. Or maybe he would a CEO of the latest company going public and all the people invest in him. Or the leader of the latest pop or rock band and young people follow him. In any case the message is the same, the relationship between Jesus and his Father in heaven. Jesus follows his Father's commands and leads his people to safety no matter what.

The power behind the image of the Good Shepherd is that the shepherd is willing to lay down his life for his sheep. Also the sheep recognise his voice and will only follow that voice. Jesus listens to the voice of his Father in heaven and acts upon what he hears. We are called to recognise the voice of Christ in our life and act upon what we have heard and follow him.

Today throughout the world we celebrate vocation Sunday and this gospel is an apt selection because I believe listening to God's voice is our vocation in life. But there is a second part to our vocation and that is acting on what we hear. Like Paul and Barnabas in today's first reading, we are called to act on what we hear. Yes, we are all called to lead a life of holiness and share our gifts for the good of others.We are called to lead this life of holiness in different ways. Some to married life, others to single and still others are called to lead it in a more intense way as ordained or avowed religious in our church. Whatever our current life choice we need to ask ourselves: Is this the will of Christ?

Maybe you are called to an intense response, to live a religious or ordained life. But if not, we are still called to share our gifts for the good of others. Whatever the case may be, we are called to lead our Christian vocation by listening to God's voice and acting on it. And we do it together in community. Our vocation is to listen to God's voice and act on it.

---

1. In Colorado two students went to their School, Columbine High School and shot dead over 20 people and then took their own lives. This occurred a few days prior to the giving of this homily.

Love in New Ways or Love Someone New

I recently read a book entitled *The Five Love Languages*. The book is really aimed at those who have just got married and how they can keep their marriage alive with love, but I think it has some helpful hints for all of us. It speaks of the way we communicate our love for one another. The book maintains that there are five languages. There are probably more but let me focus on these five for a moment. First there are words of affirmation – words such 'I love you', 'Thank you,' 'You are awesome.' These words communicate directly how one feels. Second: quality time – spending time with your loved one, either at a movie, walking, or talking over dinner – just time together. This communicates how important the loved one is to us. Third: receiving gifts – any man knows that if he gives his wife flowers he has credits for a week … but I mean any gift, a card, a note, a small or large gift … it is the thought that counts. Fourth: acts of service – those small actions around the house or in our lives that tell the person how much we love them, such as cleaning/painting the house or cooking a meal or doing the chores for each other. Parents do this for their children when they take them everywhere. Lastly: physical touch – the touch of another human being can capture love like no other language. We all need touch. The book suggests that we all communicate our love in different ways.

In today's gospel we hear Jesus give his disciples his final command before he departs: love one another. Not only that, but he gave them an example – himself. He said, 'Love one another as I have loved you.' Yes, he gave them words of affirmation; he gave them quality time constantly as we so often hear in the gospel stories. He gave them gifts and loved them by serving them consistently. And of course he loved them by physical touch when he healed people.

Jesus gave us the exemplar in how to love and communicate it. I have do doubt that every person in this church today loved someone, somewhere at some time. The question becomes how do we express that love and do we need to learn to communicate it in a new way? Or do we need to love someone new? I think we ought to challenge ourselves to learn new ways to express our love for one another. Can we write a note or say some words of affirmation? Can we give a gift or do something to show our love for our friends or family? Can we give someone a hug and say how much we love them today?

This week maybe we can express our love for our family and friends using some new language of love. Or maybe we can love someone new. This week maybe we love in new ways or love someone new.

Sixth Sunday of Easter:
Acts 15:1-2, 22-29; Rev 21:10-14, 22-23; Jn 14:23-29

Listen and Receive a Greater Peace

I recently saw the movie *Shrek*. It's a cartoon/animation movie that is really made for adults. (At least that is my story and I am sticking to it!) While the movie is an interesting combination of different fairytales of old, the story is new. It is a wonderful story about love. Without spoiling the movie for you, let me tell you a little about it.

The story is about Shrek, an Ogre who seeks peace in his own swampland. Remember Ogres are those green ugly beasts who eat everything in sight, including humans if given the chance. They basically scare just about everyone. However, Shrek is loveable in an odd way and when he keeps getting disturbed we feel sorry for him. One day he finds himself surrounded by all the different characters from other fairytales and his peace is completely gone. The only way to get peace is to demand it from the king. So he embarks on a journey to seek peace from the king and his only companion is a talking donkey – yes a talking donkey! The donkey refuses to stop talking and constantly challenges the Ogre to face himself. The king commands Shrek to go on a quest to rescue Princess Fiona for the king. On this quest Shrek finds true love and now has even less peace. Until he loves and allows himself to be loved he has little peace at all. Eventually he follows his heart and loves. Then he finds a greater peace than he could have ever imagined.

I think this story mirrors our own story of life. We are all in search for peace of one sort or another. And in the process, if we are open to it, we too will find love. That love often brings greater disharmony first before it brings peace. But if we allow ourselves to be loved and if we love we will find a greater peace than we ever imagined.

In today's gospel we hear Jesus promise his disciples the gift of the Holy Spirit, and he said he gives them peace greater than the world can imagine. We believe we have the gift of the Holy Spirit within us, we are temples of the Holy Spirit. And the peace that God promises is our free gift if we can respond to his love. It is the Holy Spirit that invites us on that journey (of faith) for peace. It is the Holy Spirit that guides us on that journey. In the movie, Shrek is accompanied by the talking donkey who is constantly giving him advice for the journey. In the much the same way we are accompanied by the Holy Spirit and he constantly gives us advice for our journey of life, our quest for peace. And if we heed the advice of our talking donkey, our conscience and Holy Spirit, then we too will find love and receive a greater peace than we can ever imagine.

However, we have to be open to the gift of the Holy Spirit. We need to listen to the whispering voice of God in our hearts, our conscience. We have to be willing to embark on that journey and seek God's peace. So where do we start?

Before we can love someone else, we ought to find ourselves lovable. Like Shrek in the movie, we need to accept ourselves the way we are, the ugly and the beautiful, the good and the bad, our strengths and our weaknesses. We all have weaknesses and strengths. We all have ugly parts as well as beautiful parts. But when we accept ourselves as we are then we are ready to love and be loved.

God invites us on the journey of peace and love through his Holy Spirit. On that journey we discover who we really are and come to know God even more. In the process, we find a greater peace than we could have ever imagined. To do this we need to spend some time listening to that 'talking donkey' within us, the Holy Spirit who guides us at all times.

This week maybe we take an extra 10 minutes a day and listen to the guidance of the Holy Spirit and discover and accept who we really are. In so doing we will receive a greater peace than we ever imagined. Let God disturb our peace this week so he can give us an even greater peace.

The Ascension of the Lord:
Acts 1:1-11; Eph 1:17-23; Lk 24:46-53

Fully Alive in the One Spirit

A pizza delivery man was pounding frantically on the back gate of the Vatican, 'Let me in,' he cried, 'I have a pizza for the pope and it's getting cold.' But no one answered. 'Please, someone let me in,' he shouted all the louder. Finally, a tiny opening as the solid, iron gate creaked and a cranky looking guard growled at him, 'I'll let you in, if you give me half of the tip the pope gives you.' The man quickly agreed, 'Anything, just let me deliver the pizza to the pope.' So the gate was opened and the man delivered his pizza. On the way out the guard reminded the delivery man about their agreement, 'You have not forgotten – I want half the tip!' 'With pleasure,' smiled the delivery man, who raised his hand and gave exactly one half ... of a papal blessing![1]

There are certain things in life that are still okay in half measures. For example, half a loaf of bread is better than none. A half of a glass of milk is better than none, or a half a gallon of gas is better than none. And a half of a million dollars is good at any time. But the most important things in life are not much good in half measures!

For example, what if you say to your spouse I will love you half of the time or for half of my life. Or as a friend I say I will be there for you only half of the time, or I am half committed to you as friend. Or to our children we said we'll love you half of the time. None of those are much good in half measures!

Relationships are not half measures. Relationship is a full commitment. And the same is true of our relationship with God. God wants our full commitment. Now that does not mean perfection but commitment.

In today's gospel we hear from the conclusion of the gospel of Luke and we also hear from the beginning of the Acts of the Apostles. These books are written by the same author. The Acts of the Apostles is the sequel to the gospel of Luke. In both of these sections Luke is bridging the story of Jesus to the story of the apostles. He tells how Christ instructs them with the gift of the Holy Spirit. In the Acts of the Apostles, the disciples are gazing into the sky after Jesus' ascension. They are awoken from the gaze and told to go and do the work of the Lord. They are instructed to go and preach the good news and follow the example that Christ gave them. They were to be fully alive in the Spirit. There was no half-measure here.

We too are called to live the gospel values fully. We are invited to drink fully of the cup of salvation and live fully in the Spirit. So the question is how do we live more fully in the Spirit. Each of us will find different ways to do it but perhaps we can begin at home. To live fully in the Spirit might mean talking to neighbours whom we never talk to because they are different from us. Maybe it means spending time with someone at work who is depressed or despondent about their life. Maybe it means spending more time with our children who are desperately craving our love and attention. Or maybe it is something in this community. Maybe we can participate more fully in this community by volunteering some time to those in need. Whatever it is, we are called to live fully in the one Spirit. Today and this week maybe we can partake more fully by our actions and so live in no half-measures. Today may we all be truly alive in the one Spirit and others can see the good that we do and offer praise to God.

1. Msgr Dennis Clark, *Sunday Morning: Food for the Soul*, (Rancho Santa Fe, CA: The Church of The Nativity, 1999) 264-265.

Witness to his Presence

Someone once called a priest to say that he wanted to join the parish. He went on to explain, however, that he did not want to have to go to Mass every Sunday, study the bible, be a Lector or Eucharistic Minister, visit the sick, or help out as a sponsor for candidates or catechumens. The priest commended the man for his desire to be a member of the parish, but told him that the church he wanted was located across town. The man took the directions and hung up. When he arrived at the address the priest gave him, he came face to face with the logical conclusion of his own apathetic attitude. For there stood an abandoned church and several other buildings, all boarded up and ready for demolition.[1]

The priest in this little story sent more than a subtle message. But when we think about it, the priest is right. If we want a church with no obligations, no burdens, no demands then all we want is an empty building with no life in it. Or maybe we want to have a couple of things but we want little or no obligation put on us. It seems to me that we may have church on our terms but we do not have church as God intended.

In today's first reading of the Acts of the Apostles, Stephen is filled with the Holy Spirit and he sees the glory of God. He testifies to the presence of Christ in the world and in response they stone him to death. Stephen's response to these people who do him violence is an indispensable Christian witness: 'Lord, do not hold this sin against them.' We see in Stephen the ideal Christian response to violence.

We do not fight violence with violence.[2] Instead we are called to forgive. We are asked to witness to Christ's presence in our lives in the same way that Stephen witnessed to it in his life. Most of us will not be required to give up our life. Hopefully none of us will be martyred for our faith. But maybe we are asked to give up something else that does not witness to Christ's presence in our lives such as the destructive habits of seeking power and money at all costs. Maybe we need to give up the image of church we have and volunteer for ministries in the parish and community. Maybe we need to give up our image of ourselves and not worry about how we look or how we sound. Maybe we are to witness to Christ by our willingness to forgive others, especially when we know we are right like Stephen. Yes, our lives ought to be a living testimony of how much we love God. So 'church' is more than a building or collection of buildings. It is a coming together of the people of God. When we gather around this table in Christ's name and remember what he has done for us, we share our gift of witness to one another and to Christ. Church is the 'people of God' witnessing to God's presence among them.

Like the man asking the priest for a parish without commitments, we sometimes ask for a discipleship without commitments. There is no such thing. So where do we witness and how? We know we witness to his presence by more than coming to Mass but it requires our dedication throughout the day and week ahead. Maybe we can witness to Christ by calling a friend or neighbour and forgiving them their offence against us. Whatever it is, let's make one new commitment right now and bear witness to Christ today.

1. Brian Cavanaugh, *Sower's Seeds Aplenty*, (Mahwah, New Jersey: Paulist Press, 1996) #23.
2. William F. Maestri, *Grace Upon Grace*, (Makati, Philippines: St Paul Publications, 1988) p 256.

Pentecost Sunday:
Acts 2:1-11; 1 Cor 12:3-7, 12-13; Jn 20:19-23

Favourite Hiding Place

When I was a child I had a favourite hiding place. It was my parents' bed. I would go there when it was dark and I was alone in the house. Indeed, anytime that I was afraid. When I was there, I felt safe and secure. I felt comforted by the silence. It was my hiding place! After a while my parents would put me into my own bed and all would be fine.

When you were young, did you have a favourite hiding place? Did you have somewhere to go when you felt afraid? Maybe it was your parents' bed or maybe it was under a table or in the closet. Wherever it was, remember that feeling of safety and security? Well in today's scripture we hear about the apostles in their hiding place – the upper room. They were afraid. So they came together and hid to feel safe and secure. But it was in this moment of weakness and vulnerability that Christ came to them and gave them his greatest gift – the Holy Spirit.

The Holy Spirit is depicted by Luke, the author of Acts, as being 'like a strong, driving wind' or like 'tongues as of fire' representing passion and courage. They were immediately 'on fire' with the Spirit and readily preached the gospel to all. Everyone could hear in their own individual language. Elsewhere in scripture God's Spirit is depicted as a 'dove' (Lk 3:22) or as a burning bush but not consumed (Ex 3:2) and even as a tiny whispering sound. While these are attractive symbols I believe the ancient Irish had it right, when it came to the Holy Spirit. In the Celtic imagination, the Holy Spirit is not a pure and peaceful dove, but a wild goose. Yes, a wild goose! You see geese are wild and uncontrollable; they make lots of noise with their honking and they will bite anyone who tries to contain them. They fly faster in flocks than on their own. In a sense they are guard dogs.[1]

When in fear we go to our hiding places and if we are open to God's Spirit he will minister to us. He will give us the gift of his Spirit and set us on fire. We too are called to be like the apostles, preaching and acting out the gospel. We are called to be like wild geese, honking the good news of the gospel. To 'honk' when we see injustice. 'Honk' when someone's rights are deprived. 'Honk' when we experience the needs of the poor and oppressed. 'Honk' when life is not preserved or respected. Yes, this week we are called to be open to God's Spirit. We are called to leave our hiding places and 'honk' wildly, to be uncontainable, speak for justice and fight for what is right.

1. Patricia Datchuk Sanschez, *Celebration: An Ecumenical Worship Resource*, (Kansas City, MO: National Catholic Reporter Company, Inc., June 3, 2001).

Trinity Sunday:
Prov 8:22-31; Rom 5:1-5; Jn 16:12-15

Love like the Trinity: Learn Someone's Name

In nearly every household throughout the world the same person visits the same house almost every day. That person often comes and goes yet most people hardly see him/her come or go. Most days that person gives us gifts, but some days s/he gives us challenges. That person is always there for us no matter what the weather, cold or hot, snow or sun, wet or dry, hail or heat, s/he is always there. Does anyone know who I am talking about?

It is the mail carrier or postman I used to know as a child. Yes, every day they deliver mail. They come and go from the same household day after day and yet, how many of us do not know their names? This week, I found out our mailman's name is Peter, and he is married with several children, one of whom is sick this week. It has taken me almost a year to find out his name. It is amazing that the same person comes to our house every day and yet, most of us do not know their name. We all like to be called by our name. We all like to be known for who we really are.

Today we celebrate the Feast of the Holy Trinity. We make note of the central mystery of our Christian faith. We name the persons of the Trinity – Father, Son, and Holy Spirit. Not that God's name is Father or the Holy Spirit's name Holy Spirit, but we recognise who they are and how they work in our lives.

Today we say explicitly what we say implicitly at every liturgical celebration, we believe in one God who is Father, Son, and Holy Spirit. It is our Catholic tradition that we start every liturgy with the sign of the cross, in the name of the Father, Son, and Holy Spirit and we close every liturgy with a blessing in the name of the Father, Son, and Holy Spirit. We remind ourselves to have God the Father in our minds, and God the Son, Jesus Christ in our hearts, and God the Holy Spirit throughout our whole body. Finally when we join our hands it symbolises our unity with God the Father, Son and Holy Spirit whose communion is a sign of love.

In one sense, understanding the Trinity is beyond us, because understanding fully who God is, is beyond us. God is in-

effable (no words can fully express who God is.) Yet, we can experience God fully. Yes, it is true. Explaining the mystery of the
Trinity is difficult, but we can still experience God.

St Augustine images the Trinity in a helpful way. He maintains that the Father is the Lover, Jesus is the beloved, and the
Holy Spirit is the love flowing between Father and Son. So, we
can experience God by participating in love. When we love, we
can know God. When we are loved and allow ourselves to be
loved, we experience the power of God at work in the world.

Today's scripture gives us further insight to this. In the first
reading from the book of Proverbs, we hear about Wisdom – the
Holy Spirit, which is God's playful companion in creating the
universe. Then in the gospel, we hear Jesus tell us that God the
Father and he are one and he will give us the Holy Spirit who
will reveal it to us. In other words, the Father and the Son love
each other, and the Holy Spirit is that flow of love between
them.

So if we are to participate more fully in the Trinity, we can
love like the Father, or we can allow ourselves to be loved like
the Son, or we can be love itself like the Holy Spirit. The question
is, how can we do this?

Let me suggest one way we can do it this week. Maybe we
can learn the name of someone new this week. Maybe it is our
neighbour, whom we see every day, but we cannot remember
their name. Maybe it is the receptionist at work whom we pass
every day without knowing their name. Maybe it is the clerk at
the store or the waiter at the restaurant. Whoever it is, let us
promise to learn someone's name this week.

And in so doing, we love like the Father.

The Body of Christ is always in Need

A young woman came to me recently complaining about the Catholic Church. She said, 'You know, Father, the problem with the Catholic Church is that it's always asking for something and it's usually money!' A little taken back by the statement and the indisputable truth of it, I wondered what I could say. Then I remembered the story I heard given by the president of Miami University at their commencement celebration.

He recalled when he and his wife had a little boy – their first-born. He was a delight to their hearts, but he was always costing them something. When he was very young he needed to be nursed and constantly held as well as forever changing his diapers. Then when he was older he needed clothing, shoes, food and education. He also had special needs. In all of this they gladly provided for him as he was their son. Then one day the little boy died. He no longer cost a dollar but their boy was dead.[1]

I hope none of you ever experience the loss of your son or daughter. Every need is a sign of life. Body, mind and soul have their needs and they must be met continually.

A community that is constantly in need of funds is alive and growing. A dead community has no need and we will not bother anyone.

Today we celebrate the Solemnity of the Body and Blood of Christ. As we recognise the presence of Christ in the elements of the bread and wine, we are encouraged also to recognise the presence of Christ in each other as we gather as *the* Body of Christ. So when we receive the Body and Blood of Christ in this celebration we will say Amen to what we receive and also Amen to who we are – the Body of Christ.

That body is very much alive in this community. As any body that is alive it has needs. There are those among us who are in dire need physically but we would never know unless we were involved in their lives. There are others among us here today who are emotionally starving and are in need of any loving affection. Then there are others of us who are spiritually starving and even this eucharist will leave them in hunger. Yes, there are many among us in need because this Body of Christ is

69

alive indeed. It is the sign of our life and vitality. Today we can celebrate what we receive by our Amen and so we can also celebrate who we are as the Body of Christ. The Body is always in need because we are alive.

1. James S. Hewett, *Illustrations Unlimited*, (Wheaton, Illinois: Tyndale House Publishers, Inc., 1988) 348.

Water to Wine? Jesus can transform us too!

Today's readings provide a virtual cornucopia of ideas from which to preach. It is a preacher's delight. Well, I want to focus on the miracle at Cana and how it comes about.

This is the first miracle of Jesus and it is the start of Jesus' public ministry. In John's gospel it is called a 'sign', the biblical word that points to the wonder-worker God and it is the beginning of the Book of Signs. It is interesting to note that Jesus' mother simply states 'They have no more wine.' However, this seemingly innocuous statement contains an implicit request or prayer to solve their problem. Jesus picks up on this and says it is no concern of his, his time has not yet come! But Mary believes in her Son Jesus and so she instructs the servants to do whatever he tells them.

The miracle of changing water into wine becomes a great symbol of life for us. Jesus not only transforms the water into wine but he does so in great quantity. He not only listens to his Mother's request/prayer but he answers her in abundance. Jesus promises to do the same for us if only we would ask as his mother did.

Let's examine our lives for minute and look for the similarity to this story. How often have we heard a simple statement like, 'They are all out of wine.' I mean that metaphorically, not a party scene. Although I am sure that we have heard it at dinner parties too. I mean it in the sense of what we Americans often call the honeymoon period. And then someone says 'The honeymoon is over.' In other words the good times are over and we are back to the joyless part of life.

It seems that when everything is going well in our lives, there is joy and excitement and even festivity. Then something happens, there is a change, whether radical or gradual, and life becomes dull and boring. We like school but now the exams are here it is tough work. We like work but the job has become too stressful and arduous. We love being married but my spouse has changed and somewhere along the line the zest for the marriage is gone. The wine has run out.

Or maybe it was something more radical. We were living

71

happily and then we got very sick and life is tiresome and un-bearable. The wine ran out!

Things were fine and then our spouse died, or our child died, or even our best friend died, and the wine ran out.

Whether radical or gradual, there are times in our lives that we look in the mirror and say 'I have no more wine.' Others too have the same challenge in their lives. This is the exact point when Jesus comes along and says I can not only change the water into wine but I can transform your life. Not in some Pollyanna sense – where everyone is smiling and pretending the pain is gone – but in a real and permanent way.

He can transform the pain and betrayal into growth and ful-fillment. He will make all things new if we allow his power to work in our lives. Do we really believe that? And if so how does God work that miracle?

This brings me to the second part of the Cana miracle – the servants. Without them there would be no miracle! In their sim-ple ordinary actions Jesus made something extraordinary hap-pen. He transformed an ordinary jug of water into a vintage wine. They followed his instructions even though they could not see the reason. They participated in the miracle by doing some-thing very ordinary. So we are called to act in the same way as Mary in asking for miracles/signs and act like the servants in doing the ordinary things of life for others. Miracles can happen for us and others if we co-operate with God.

There are lots of people we know who are content with water. But Jesus promises us wine, the symbol of joy. There are others we know who have broken hearts and are in pain – physical, mental, emotional, and certainly spiritual – they need and seek a miracle in their lives. We can play an important role in their lives by doing the ordinary things with great joy in our hearts.

Maybe this week we can ask God to help us or others in prayer as Mary did. Or we can act as the servants of the gospel today and do the ordinary things of life, knowing that God has a plan for us and others. We ought to actively seek to do God's will in our lives. How about inviting someone who we know is hurting into a conversation and in so doing bring healing? Maybe we can invite someone who is spiritually hurting to join us at church some week?

This week we can stretch out to someone who is hurting and be part of their miracle and transform our own lives.

Judge Nobody

Yesterday was a very important day in the United States of America. We had the inauguration of a new President – George W. Bush. As part of that event we heard an inauguration speech that will go down in history for good or bad. Yesterday he put forward his programme for change – to unify the nation. Indeed he will be measured against what he said in his campaign but more so in what he said today as he starts his presidency.

In the gospel of Luke we also hear of another inaugural speech. We hear the inaugural speech of Jesus Christ as he begins his public ministry. His words are stark and unadorned:[1] Jesus came in the power of the Spirit to make things better for the poor, to set prisoners free, to restore sight to the blind, to proclaim a year of favour from the Lord. This is the programme that Jesus Christ promises to bring about in his ministry.

But Jesus goes one step further. He says that it is now fulfilled in your hearing. Jesus assures us in him this is fulfilled. Today Jesus tells us the same. Today this is fulfilled in our hearing. Today somehow God is breaking through. The question is, how is God breaking through?

Maybe we can take a lead from Paul's letter to the Corinthians. Last week we heard Paul tell them of the variety of gifts they have, all given from the same Spirit. And today we hear Paul encourage the Corinthians in their diversity. He tells them that they are still part of the same body – the Body of Christ. This is both a metaphor and reality. We are like a body in parts and gifts/talents and each of us needs each other. But we also are the Body of Christ, together we are part of Christ's mystical body. But we also need to accept our diversity.

We are very aware of our diversity each time we gather here for worship. We celebrate our diversity here at church and we ought to. We may come from different races or ethnic backgrounds: Filipino, Vietnamese, Hispanic, African, Indian, Pakistani, Irish, Polish, Native Americans. We may come from different political camps (Republican, Democrat); economic backgrounds; age groups; education (with framed advanced or professional degrees in their offices or barely able to sign their names). The list could go on. The differences may be what first strike us as we enter here but as we pray together those differences melt away into a unity. And Paul says that is the real basis for our unity.

We are celebrating Christian Unity Week. In the same way that we are different from one another before we pray and then come closer in prayer, we have many differences with other Christian Churches but when we pray to the same Lord Jesus Christ we come closer if we allow it to work within us. So this week let us pray for our Christian brothers and sisters who worship at other churches that one day we will be united in prayer, together at the same table as Christ intended it.

Let me suggest one way of bringing this about unity and having God's word fulfilled in our hearing. Let me invite you this week to celebrate a Day of Acceptance. I mean that we choose one day this week and say 'Today I will not judge anyone. I will accept everyone and everything the way God intended. I will look beyond the surface of colour, race, age, language, or church affiliation and instead see the child of God whom Jesus promises to save.'

This week we can fulfill this reading in our hearing and participate in bringing Jesus' inaugural address to fulfillment. We can recognise the unity in our diversity by accepting those around us.

1. Monika K. Hellwig, *Gladness Their Escort*, (Wilmington, Delaware: Michael Glazier, Inc., 1987) 337.

Be a Prophet: Tell the Truth!

We humans are unique creatures. We can remember events in our lives and reflect on them for learning and understanding. It is interesting to see how far back we can remember. Some people can remember a long way back, others only a few years. What is the first childhood memory you have? Is it around your teenage years, when you were young and free? Or is it when you were a little child running around like a mop on the floor? Usually we can remember back as far as three years old and seldom can we remember back past that. However, our parents can typically remember our whole childhood. They can tell us the silly little things we did as young boys or girls. Most of our parents remember all of our lives, especially the early years. They remember because they loved us as best as they could and those years were evidence of that love.

Well, in today's first reading from the Prophet Jeremiah we hear God tell Jeremiah that he knew him before he was formed in the womb. Not only did God know him but he knew him before he was born. God loved Jeremiah and knew him intimately from the beginning. And God chose him for a special mission. He chose him to be a prophet. God told Jeremiah that even though his mission was difficult, he would always be there for him. God wanted Jeremiah to realise how much he loved him. God would never abandon Jeremiah no matter what because he loves him so.

God is telling us the same thing. We are all known by God before we were born. He loves each and every one of us and he has a mission for us. Each one of us is called to be a prophet like Jeremiah. When we think of prophets we often think of people who foretell the future, often predicting death and calamity. But in the bible, prophets are people who tell the truth. They tell the truth about what God has done in our lives, what he continues to do, and what he will do in the future for us. Prophets are bearers of the truth.

It is not always easy to be a bearer of the truth. Look at what happened to Jesus in today's gospel. His own people wanted to throw him off a cliff and kill him. He said he came to heal the sick, forgive sinners and give all the good news of the kingdom of God. But that truth got him in trouble. Maybe this week we can tell the truth in all we do. Maybe we can be honest about things that happen. Maybe we can be bearers of the truth in every day life. Whether it is at school, work or at home, telling the truth is not always easy. Sometimes we will be persecuted for it. Other times we will be lauded for it.

This week, maybe we can tell the truth in all ways and in so doing be a prophet to those around us.

Fifth Sunday in Ordinary Time:
Is 6:1-8; 1 Cor 15:1-11; Lk 5:1-11

Here I am Lord!

Several years ago, I returned to Trinity College, Dublin, the university I attended in Ireland as an undergraduate and walked through the campus for nostalgic reasons. I walked in the department of Computer Science to see how it changed since I attended. As I walked into the offices someone shouted, 'Brendan'. I was shocked that anyone would remember my name. It was the secretary to the Head of the Department, Professor Bryne. She remembered my name and I was most impressed! It had been fifteen years since we last met. Then she said that the Professor would be delighted to see me. I protested saying, 'The Professor will not remember me.' At that same moment, in walked Professor Byrne responding, 'Brendan McGuire, I thought I recognised your voice. How are you doing in California?' I was totally taken back! Not only did he remember me by name but he also knew where and what I was doing. I must admit I felt great to walk into my old school 15 years later and still be remembered by name and voice. The reality was that Professor Byrne was a kind and gentle man who took great pleasure in remembering people by name. He took interest in people's lives.

I am sure at some time in the past someone you have not seen in a long time greeted you by name and remembered who you are. Remember how that made you feel. We like to be called by our names and be remembered for who we are.

Well God not only knows our names, he knows us through and through because he created us in the womb. He knew us before we were even born. God has a plan for each one of us but he allows us to discover that plan for ourselves. That is the journey of life. It is not a game but a discovery of who we are called to be. Discovery of who we are called to be by name!

In today's first reading we hear how Isaiah discovers his call to be a prophet. He considers himself unworthy but the Lord reminds him that he decides who is worthy and gives him the gift to speak as a prophet.

In the second reading, we hear Paul tell the Corinthians that he is what he is (a prophet and disciple) only by the grace of

God. God called him by name despite his feeling of unworthiness.

Finally, in the gospel, we hear Jesus call the first disciples, Simon Peter, Andrew, James and John. He called these fishermen all by name asking them to become fishers of men.

Each of these passages shares a different story of vocation. But each one shares the common story of God knowing us by name. Not only does our God know us by name but he also has a plan for each one of us. If we could only realise for a minute the profound gift that our God is a personal God who cares for you and me. Not just some transcendent God in the sky but a real person who is present in our world. If we can allow that reality to enter into our hearts then our prayer will become a genuine listening session where we can discover the path specially chosen for us.

If we are honest with ourselves, then we will feel overwhelmed when God asks us to do something. In other words, like Simon Peter or Isaiah, when we hear God call our name we feel unworthy to do his work. We might ask, why me? I am not good at this or that. Yet he calls each one of us uniquely to do his work in the world. Today's scripture urges us to respond like Isaiah and Peter and say, 'Here I am, Lord, send me!'

Even though we might be sinful and weak, the Lord still calls us to do his work in our world. Today and this week maybe we can spend some time listening to God direct our thoughts and actions. Maybe we hear God call us by name and know that God is a God who loves us and know that God is a God who calls us to be his disciple in this world in our lives today.

'Here I am, Lord, send me!'

Sixth Sunday in Ordinary Time:
Jer 17:5-8; 1 Cor 15:12, 16-20; Lk 6:17, 20-26

Which Wolf Do You Feed?

There is a story told of an old Cherokee talking with his grandson. 'Two wolves are warring inside me,' he said. 'One is evil. He speaks of greed, envy, lust, deceit, and power. The other is good. He speaks of love, forgiveness, patience, self-sacrifice, kindness, and generosity. The battle rages within me. It rages within you, too, and inside every person.' The grandson thought for a moment and said, 'But Grandpa, which wolf will win?' The old Cherokee answered with great conviction, 'The one you feed.'[1]

There is a battle inside all of us. The battle to do good or to do evil. The battle to listen to the voice of God or to listen to the voice of self-indulgence. Be assured the battle is always on even though there are times we think everything is fine. The battle is often a subtle fight. A fight that seems to have no significance. 'Nobody will know notice,' we often counsel ourselves. 'Nobody sees the difference,' we can think. 'I do not need God. I can do this on my own,' we convince ourselves. However, deep within our hearts we know the difference and we know God knows.

Often those moments are turning points in the battle between good and evil in our lives. But we have to recognise that every decision is significant. Every choice we make tells us something about ourselves. Every choice can be a decision guided by God.

Today's first reading are words from God through the prophet Jeremiah warning the people of the day, and us, that we ought to rely on God alone. We must not put our trust in humans but solely in God. If we do so the Lord tells us that we will bear great fruit. We will be like a tree planted alongside a river, never worrying about water or nourishment. So too we are called to plant ourselves beside the Lord and never worry about our spiritual nourishment. We are called to put our trust in God alone.

This is not easy in today's world when there are so many other things demanding our attention. We love our sports and spend many hours playing or watching. We love our television and we spend so many hours absorbing its programmes. We love our computers and spend endless hours on the Internet.

Evil does not come dressed as evil. Evil always comes looking attractive and seductive. Good people are not tempted by
evil. Good people are tempted by evil disguised as good. I am
not saying that sports, television, computer, or even the Internet
are evil. But like the Cherokee giving advice to his grandson in
the story, whatever we give our time and energy to will domi-
nate us. Whatever we feed within us will live! Thus if we use the
sports or television as an escape from our duties as husband or
wife, child or parent, student or worker, then that is what we
will achieve – escape. If we use our computer or the Internet to
satisfy our childless desires such as playing endless games or
looking at pornography then that is what we will achieve – self-
indulgence. We are feeding the evil wolf within us. We are not
listening to the Lord or trusting in God.

Instead we are called to hope in the Lord at all times. We are
called to plant ourselves close to the Lord by doing good for others and listening to the guidance of the Lord. We are called to
spend our time and energy in doing good.

If necessary we are called to even suffer for the Lord.
According to the gospel today, if we do so, then the Lord assures
us that we will be 'happy'. We will be happy insofar as the Lord
will care for us and we will be content doing the Lord's will.

Maybe we can be generous with our time this week to others
and be patient and kind as they outline their struggles in life. It
is what we spend our time on that will determine what we do. It
is how we spend our time that will determine whether we do
good or evil. The battle between good and evil within us always
wages. The battle of the wolves will always be present, but we
can feed the good wolf within us by trusting in God and doing
good for others.

So today, which wolf will we feed?

1. *Homily Helps*, (St Anthony Messenger Press: Cincinnati, OH), June 25,
2003.

Beyond Quid Pro Quo

There is an old Latin adage, *quid pro quo*,[1] that means to do onto others ... It speaks of the relationship between doing something for someone and that someone doing something for you in return. The modern equivalent is probably 'You scratch my back and I will scratch yours.' In my prior business experience I found that this was the unwritten rule of business. 'If you do something for me then I will do something for you.' It makes good business sense to look after those who look after you. For example, if a customer likes to spend money in the store then that customer is given preferential treatment. It is simply good business sense.

Being a Christian is more than good business sense. We are called not only to be good to our friends but also called to be good to those we consider 'not' our friends. It makes good sense to be loving toward our family members and friends because they are supportive of us in our time of need. They are there for us and we are there for them. These relationships are very important to us and we ought to treat our families and friends well.

However, the gospel calls us to go beyond this adage of doing good to those who do good to us. Being Christian is more than good business sense. The gospel tells us today that, yes, we are to 'treat others as you would like to be treated'. But we are also invited to go beyond this *quid pro quo*.

As Christians, we are called to not judge or condemn others but 'to be compassionate as our Father is compassionate.' The question then becomes how can we be compassionate? Compassion here refers to being generous to others – generous not only with our material possessions but also with our forgiveness.[2] We are not given any options here: as Christians we are commanded to be generous as Christ was generous. So we have to ask ourselves how we can be generous in new ways.

All we have is God's gifts to us and how we share those gifts is our gift to God. We can share our material possessions with not just our family and friends but also with our neighbours, co-workers, and strangers. We can do this in small ways such as offering to buy lunch or dinner on occasion. Or maybe we can offer to shop for an elderly or sick neighbour. Or maybe we can give a portion of income to charity so that those who are strangers can be fed or given home.

We are also commanded to be generous with our forgiveness of others. It seems that this is one of the hardest things for us to do. We can give away our material possessions more easily than forgiving. So where do we start? I think the best place to start is to look at our own lives. Most of us are aware of our sinfulness and how God forgives us. He initially forgave us and welcomed us to his table. We are motivated by God's forgiveness of us first. Then we are asked to pass on this generosity in forgiveness to others.

So this week maybe we can forgive someone, especially someone who is not good to us in return. In today's gospel Christ tells us that the base level is *quid pro quo* – 'the amount you measure out is the amount that will be measured back to you.'

This week we can be generous with our material possessions but even more so with our forgiveness and move beyond *quid pro quo*.

1. Adapted from Reginald H. Fuller, *Preaching the Lectionary: The Word of God for the Church Today*, (Collegeville, Minnesota: The Liturgical Press, 1984) 466.
2. Adapted from William F. Maestri, *Grace Upon Grace*, (Makati, Philippines: St Paul Publications, 1988) 272.

Introspect not Project

I have a friend who is a priest and psychologist and we love to go back and forth in conversation about our ministries. He always warns me to watch what I say. He tells me that I should really listen to what I say about others. He informs me that we often talk about ourselves even though we think we are talking about others. In other words, he cautions me to be slow to judge others. For example, I have a bad habit of being late for meetings. But you know what? When I am actually on time, guess what? I expect others to be on-time and sometimes I complain, 'Why are people always late?' A little inconsistent. Yes! And that is only a minor example.

The technical psychological term for this is 'projection'. We project on to others the very weakness we ourselves suffer from. And then we often judge others harshly. Who among us does not know someone who is great at gossip? They seem to know everything about everyone. Then one day there is some gossip about them and they are horrified. They complain, 'How could people destroy people's lives like that?' Excuse me! What have they been doing for years?

But the gospel calls us to not project but introspect – to take a look at our own lives and see if we are consistent, to see if we are hypocritical, as Jesus says. And so we are called to reflect on our lives regularly in order to know ourselves better. Then we will be up to the challenge of the gospel. Socrates, the ancient Greek philosopher, once said that 'an unexamined life is not worth living.' So where do we begin?

Some people say we are what we do. While that is true it is not everything we are. For example, are we any less human if we cannot work? I mean let us say that our mother, father or child is sick and cannot work or do anything, are they any less our parent or child? Of course not! So we are more than what we do. Some say that we are what we say. Indeed today's first reading from the book of Sirach says beware of speaking because people will know who we are when we speak.

I think that is true but it is not it all. For example each week I come here and give homilies. You all hear me speak and have come to know me. When I speak like this I share a bit of who I am. Is that all there is to me? Do you all know me completely? No. There is more to me than this too.

Others say that we are what we think. If we think that we are good then we are. Or if we think good thoughts then we are there. Of course we know that there is more to it than thinking. We are all here in church thinking rather piously now. But how easily all this could change! For example, let us imagine that we are all lining up to receive communion, the music is playing in the background and there is a quiet and serene atmosphere. Then out of the blue a child starts screaming uncontrollably and running up and down the aisle pulling at everyone. Unless you are different from me, you would be thinking 'Where are the parents? Have they gone home?' Yet we have no idea how difficult the life of the parents could be right now. Maybe they have lost a relative this week or maybe they are overwhelmed with life and figure 'It is the Lord's house. I can relax now!' How quickly our pious thoughts can fly out the window. So it is not just thoughts either.

Let me suggest we are who we are in all three – our actions, words, and thoughts. We are called to integrate them to make ourselves better Christians. And the only way we can do that is to reflect on our lives. We are called to introspect not project.

So this week maybe we can set aside some extra time to reflect on our lives. This week we can introspect instead of project.[1]

---

1. Jude Siciliano, OP, *Preachers Exchange*, (Raleigh, NC: preachex@opsouth.org). Socrates B. Villegas, *Only Jesus Always Jesus*, (Manila, Philippines: Anvil Publishing, Inc., 1997) pp 2-4.

Keep the Fire of Faith Burning

A pastor of a busy parish went to visit an old time parishioner who was no longer attending Mass on Sundays. As he knocked on the door, the parishioner greeted the pastor coolly suspecting that the pastor was there for money. 'Good afternoon, Father.' 'Good afternoon, Mr Jones. I came to chat a little,' the pastor answered. 'Well come in for a cup of tea, then,' said Mr Jones. It was a cold wintry day and they sat next to the fire. As Mr Jones poured the tea the silence was deafening. Then the pastor leaned towards the fire and took the tongs, pulling out one of the coals and placing it on the hearth of the fire. At first it continued to burn brightly but soon it dimmed to an ashen colour and slowly burned out. The parishioner sat back and spoke clearly. 'Okay, Father, I'll be at Mass on Sunday.' That Sunday the pastor and his community warmly welcomed back the old time parishioner.[1]

The parishioner understood the subtle message of the pastor – like a coal burning in the fire surrounded by other coals – we need to be surrounded by other believers to keep our faith burning brightly. Separate from our community of believers we can remain aflame for only a short time before the fire of our faith seems to dim a little. Coming to Mass on Sundays may seem like a burden or may be done out of obligation, but in reality coming together with other people of faith keeps our faith burning brightly.

There are times that we feel that it is not necessary or helpful to go to church or attend Mass on Sundays, but if we skip for no good reason, we realise that our faith is no longer burning within us. Our faith is interdependent on our connection to other believers.

In today's first reading Solomon reminds the people that even those who are not Israelites can come to know the Lord. Solomon implores his people to accept and welcome those who want to know the Lord, especially if they are foreigners.[2] He implores them to accept others into the community of faith, allowing others to burn brightly with the fire of faith.

In the second reading today St Paul chastises the Galatians

for their intolerance of new believers. A certain group of Galatians called the Judaisers – Jewish Christians who impose the Mosaic Law on the Gentiles who want to become Christians – are making it difficult for people to become believers. Paul challenges this practice and demands that they be hospitable to new believers, to welcome the strangers among them, allowing them to become aflame with faith.

The centurion in today's gospel acts in faith even though he is not part of the Jewish religion. Jesus sends a clear message of welcome to this new believer by healing his servant and praising his faith.

When we have a tight community of believers it is easy to appear unwelcoming to others trying to believe in God. Instead we are called to welcome all into our community. We are called to burn brightly with faith ourselves, so that others may see the fire in our community and feel welcome to come and join us. This means that we are called to welcome back those who have strayed from the faith, especially those who have grievances with our church. This means we are called to welcome into our community those who are not like us, especially those from different countries or ethnicities. This means that we must be willing to examine the way we do things, especially the way we invite others into community gatherings.

As people of faith, we know we need each other in community to keep our faith burning brightly. And so the challenge then for us today is to welcome everyone from the coldness of unbelief and into the fire of faith, leaving no one as a stranger.

---

1. Brian Cavanaugh, *Fresh Packet of Sower's Seeds*, (Mahwah, New Jersey: Paulist Press, 1994).
2. William F. Maestri, *Grace Upon Grace*, (Makati, Philippines: St Paul Publications, 1988) 275.

The Power of a Visit

When I was a child I remember once a month my parents, my brothers, sisters and I would visit by grandparents in Enniscorthy, Co Wexford. It was always a long day because as many as seven children would cram into the car for the two to three hour car journey visiting my grandparents and then three hours back. I remember those visits clearly because we did it every month without fail. Most of all I remember wrongly fearing my grandmother because she sat in the corner shaking nervously, not speaking but just staring at us children. She suffered from Parkinson's disease for 19 years and my grandfather cared for her until she died. These visits were incredibly important to me as a child, not because I enjoyed them that much, but because I learned the power of the human 'visit'.

Despite my grandfather's testy ways, my parents would always explain how difficult it is for grandpa and we would always return for another visit. Invariably grandpa would stop our conversation and listen to grandma ask a question in a voice only my grandfather could have understood. 'Lena wants to kiss the children before they go,' he would say. Each of us in turn would present ourselves and she would kiss us gently on the cheek. Then my grandma would smile brighter than life. That smile I always remember, as it made every long trip worth the effort.

The power of a human visit to those who are sick or homebound is beyond words for those who are in need. It not only can bring healing, but it can bring new life. But that is also true of any physical visit. Years ago it was common to visit neighbours and friends. Sometimes, we used to visit them to chat, sometimes for dinner or a cup of tea, but always for the human interaction. With the advent of the telephone, computers and e-mail it seems that we have lost the art of visiting one another.

In today's first reading and gospel we hear about a dead son returning to life and to the mother. However, it is the response of the widow of Zarephath and the response of the crowd at Nain that lead us to the truth, 'A great prophet has appeared among us. God has visited his people.' The word 'visit' is one of the greatest words in the bible.[1] Our God is a God who visits his people to bring salvation to all who will listen. God visited his people in Israel through the ancient prophets symbolised in today's reading by Elijah's bringing to life the dead son of the widow.

God also visited us in the person of Christ Jesus, symbolised in today's gospel by Jesus bringing to life the dead son of the widow. The truth is that God loves us so much that he became one of us, showing us the truth that God brings life out of death.

God also continues to visit us through the word and the sacraments. He comes to us at every eucharist and enables us to become food for one another. Yes, our God is a God who visits his people regularly. The question then becomes how do we respond to this visit?

One of the ways we can respond is to recognise this life-giving power of a human visit to others. Anyone who has been sick or homebound knows of the power of a physical visit of a friend or family member. It brings healing and new life. But that is also true of an ordinary human visit. I am not saying that it is wrong to use the telephone to stay in touch with others or send an e-mail to remain connected with each other's lives. Nothing, however, replaces the physical presence of a human being.

The smile on my grandmother's face reminds me of the power of the human visit. Maybe we can visit someone this week, whether it be a family member, friend or neighbour, and bring a smile to their face.

---

1. Reginald H. Fuller, *Preaching the Lectionary: The Word of God for the Church Today*, (Collegeville, Minnesota: The Liturgical Press, 1984) 475.

Acknowledge, Accept and Be Grateful

Recently I was driving across the country on vacation and while driving in Utah through a small town a scruffy man driving a beat-up old car pulled up alongside me and beckoned me to roll down my window. I was a little nervous at first because of his rough appearance and one has to be careful nowadays with road rage. However, pointing to something on his dashboard he insisted all the more. Thinking that there was something wrong with my car and he was going to help me, I rolled down my window and listened. Then he pointed at his indicator and shouted over at me, 'You are meant to use your indicator before you change lanes.' Then he drove off! I was stunned. To be honest with you, for a moment I thought of saying something like, 'Get a life!' I was ticked off that a scruffy man driving a beat-up car was giving me advice about driving. I rationalised to myself, 'Most of the time I use the indicator. I do not use the indicator only when the roads are empty or when it is obvious that I am changing lanes.' But then I thought to myself, 'Hang on a second Brendan, he is right. I should use the indicator before changing lanes at all times.' Despite his appearance he was right and his advice was right on target. Yet it was hard to take correction from such a source. Have you ever had to take correction from an unlightly source? All three readings today take up the theme of forgiveness of sin.

In the first reading the prophet Nathan confronts King David with the reality of his sin against Uriah in having him killed by sending him to the front line in their war and taking his wife as his own wife in jealousy and lust. Yes, Nathan confronted David with the reality of his sin against Uriah and against God. It was not easy for King David to be confronted by such an unlikely source. After all he was king appointed by God alone. Who was Nathan to challenge him? Prophets are those people who are willing to speak the truth of God to all who need to hear the truth. Often the first, and the most important, step in forgiveness is recognising the wrong that we have done. When confronted with the reality of his sin David acknowledges it, 'I have sinned against the Lord.' With that confession he is forgiven.

In today's second reading Paul reminds the Galatians, and us, that it is by faith in Jesus Christ and not by works that we are saved and our sins forgiven. Christ is the primary cause of our forgiveness. Paul calls us to acknowledge Christ as our Saviour and be repentant for our sins, accepting God's forgiveness through Christ and his church. Then we are called to act in gratitude like the woman in today's gospel who recognises her sinfulness and the consequent forgiveness. In gratitude to Jesus she washes, kisses, and anoints Jesus' feet. Jesus tells Simon the Pharisee that the sinful woman loves so abundantly because she fully realises that she is forgiven abundantly. She acknowledges her sinfulness first and then welcomes Christ's forgiveness with gratitude.

Like my example of the scruffy man in the beat-up car, sometimes we hear the truth from unlikely people, and it is hard to hear the truth. However, if we can look past the messenger and first acknowledge the truth of our own sinfulness and of our wrongdoing, then we will be able to accept the offer of God's forgiveness that God offers through Christ and his church. If we can just accept this forgiveness like the woman in today's gospel, then surely we can act in gratitude for that gift received.

This week maybe we can acknowledge our wrongdoing, accept the offer of Christ's forgiveness and celebrate in gratitude that gift.

Taking Up Our Cross Daily

I have a friend who is a teacher and she was once on maternity leave, missing the first two months of school. When she arrived into her new class all the students were seated in groups of three except for one student who sat alone in the corner. Inquiring from her teaching assistant as to why this student was alone, he responded, 'You will soon find out.' My friend discovered that this child was indeed a troublemaker. However, she approached the student's discipline problem in a different way than the substitute teacher. She immediately reorganised the class into groups of four, ensuring that the student no longer sat alone. Indeed she gave this particular student special attention, ensuring that he was included in every activity so that he would not regress into previous bad habits.

When I asked my friend why she went to the extra work with this one troublemaking student, she explained that once when she was young she was excluded because of her race and she remembered the pain of exclusion. She vowed that when teaching she always would find another way other than singling someone out or excluding them.

At one time or another I am sure that we have felt excluded like the student in my friend's classroom, maybe not because of our behaviour but because of who we are. It could have been when we were a student ourselves. Or maybe it was when we started a new job or moved into a new neighbourhood. Or maybe it was when we got married. At one time or another most of us have felt the pain of exclusion if only at social functions.

In today's second reading St Paul addresses the pain of exclusion. He speaks from personal experience because he was a Pharisee Jew who was now a Christian, and at first not many people believed his conversion. He was excluded from both communities, Jews and Gentiles. However, he gained his power and insight from Christ who spoke to him on the road to Damascus as his chosen apostle to all the nations. It seems that some of the Galatians were excluding others because they were Jew or Greek, or because they were slave or free, or male or female. But Paul assures the Galatians that it makes no difference now. Once we have received Christ into our lives at baptism then all barriers are broken and we all become one in Christ. Once we have experienced the forgiveness of Christ then we all become new in Christ and put on Christ.

But is that a reality in our community, namely, do we experience the reality of 'being one in Christ'? I suspect that we sometimes experience exclusion in this very community, maybe not intentional but exclusion nonetheless.

In today's gospel Peter proclaims Jesus as the Christ. While Jesus affirms that profession of faith, he also challenges Peter in an unusual way. Peter had experienced Jesus first hand, hearing him speak and seeing him heal the sick and he knew him to be Son of God, the Christ. But for Jesus being the Christ was not a dignity to be claimed as much as it was a mission to be lived out, a mission that inevitably led him to the cross. And so he responds to Peter by telling him that there is more to being a follower of Christ, a Christian, than the forgiveness of sins and a public confession of faith.

Followers of Christ are called to take up their cross every day and follow him. We, then, are called to take up that cross every day and follow him. Our cross may be exclusion from some group or exclusion from something that we want to belong to. As Christians, we are called to take up that pain of exclusion and follow Christ as we live our mission as disciples. It also means we are called not to pass our pain to others, namely we are called not to exclude others the way we are excluded. Like my friend the teacher who learnt from her pain of exclusion, we are called to learn from our pain of exclusion, our cross and give to others the experience of Christ's forgiveness by including them in our conversations and circles of friends.

Today and this week may we find a way to include the lonely in our office into our daily conversations, to include the lonely in our neighbourhood into our daily lives, to include the friendless in our midst into our circle of friends, and so live our mission as Christians by 'taking up our cross daily and following him'.

Pay It Forward

Recently I saw a movie called *Pay It Forward*. It is a story about a
7th Grade boy who responds to his Social Science class assignment of imagining a concept that will change the world. The
teacher gave the assignment to his class in an effort to have the
children think outside their own little world. However, this boy
takes the assignment very seriously and proudly proposes his
scheme called *Pay It Forward*. *Pay It Forward* as opposed to *Pay It
Back* is a scheme to change the world and I think it really can! It
proposes that a person, the boy in this case, do some extraordinary act of kindness for three people. After receiving such acts of
kindness, they pass it on to three others. The only restriction is
they cannot pay you back. Instead they must pay it forward to
three other individuals. And these actions must be extraordinary and actions that the individuals cannot do for themselves.
So you can see that 1 leads to 3, then 9, then 27, then … The
movie is about how he tries out the scheme and how difficult it
really is to actually act in such ways. The scheme works and
spreads throughout the US and the rest is left to us… What an
extraordinary scheme! I think it really could change the world.

In today's gospel we hear how Jesus turns toward Jerusalem,
symbolising his turn toward his final mission, his passion in
Jerusalem. He turns, now determined to show the way to God
and in the process Jesus tell his disciples about the cost of discipleship. We will hear in the next few weeks about how Jesus expects us to follow him. Today we hear him tell three would-be
disciples, and us, the commitment he expects of them and us.

He wants total commitment to passing on the message he has
given us. The first would-be disciple, he says, must leave everything, that 'foxes have dens and birds have nests but the Son of
Man has nowhere to lay his head.' To the second who wants to
bury his father, he says 'Let the dead bury the dead.' This person
wants to take care of his family until they die as family tradition
demanded at that time, but Jesus says now is the time to serve
the Lord. Finally, to the last would-be disciple he says that the
disciple must not turn back as a person who ploughs does not
turn back.

The message very clearly is that *now* is the time. Jesus is calling each of us to follow him now and follow his ways as he has shown us through love. The question is, how do we do it any more than we already have?

Well let me suggest that Jesus wants us to *Pay it Forward* too. He wants us to pass on the faith in some extraordinary ways. He invites us to preach the gospel to all.

So let me suggest that we take this scheme of *Pay It Forward* and let's make it real in our community. How about we choose three people and do some extraordinary act of kindness that they cannot do for themselves and have them pay it forward. Maybe as our first person we can choose someone we already are committed to like our spouse or child or best friend and pledge our love in a new and extraordinary way. The second can be someone we know from work. And let me suggest that the third person is a complete stranger.

This week, today if possible, may we commit to follow Jesus and choose three people to shower our blessings upon. May we find three people and do something for them that they cannot do for themselves.

This week let's *Pay It Forward* for Jesus and his gospel.

Never Journey Alone

Recently I had the joy of hiking in the Grand Canyon, Arizona. In every book one reads about hiking in the Grand Canyon, and indeed in the map they give you at the entrance, there is the warning to 'never hike alone'. 'Always,' it warns, 'hike in groups of two or more.' The reason for this warning is safety more than anything else. If one person falls ill or has an accident then the others can help or can get help. If, however, you are alone and something happens there is nobody to help you at 5,000 feet below the rim in temperatures of 110 degrees Fahrenheit or more. Actually when hiking on any mountain it is always rec-ommended that one hikes with at least one person in case of emergency. There is also a second and more positive reason, namely, someone with which to share the joy of the experience. For example, imagine yourself being at the base of the Grand Canyon finally reaching the Colorado River after hiking for a minimum of twelve hours in 120 degrees Fahrenheit. Now imagine that you are alone with no camera and nobody to share the experience. I am not saying you would not enjoy the experi-ence, I'm sure it would be breathtaking. However, it would be so much more meaningful to be able to share the joy with another person right there. At worst case it would be nice to be able to share the photographs with others when you return to the rim again. Yes, sharing our joys and our burdens is part of the gift of friendship or companionship on our journey of life. I am sure that we have all experienced that gift at one time or another.

In today's gospel, Jesus sends his new disciples on a journey, a journey to spread the good news of salvation to others. There is little doubt that the number 'seventy-two' is symbolic here. The mission of the Twelve represents the church's mission to Israel, symbolised by the twelve tribes of Israel; and the mission of the Seventy-Two represents its mission to the nations of the world (at this time in Israel there were believed to be seventy-two nations). But the mission was the same, to preach Jesus' own message, 'The Kingdom of God is very near to you.' The mission is characterised by a certain urgency and detachment. 'Go now' and 'take nothing with you.'

They are to trust in the Lord at all times. However, another feature of their mission is very important. Jesus sends them out two-by-two, recognising their need to rely on each other. He knows that there are not many who are willing to take the journey and they will need support for the treacherous journey ahead. 'I am sending you out like lambs among wolves.'

He knows that we need companionship on the journey of faith, to bolster us in times of weakness and to excite us in times of joy. Jesus knows we need the community of faith to help us grow. I know the concept of talking about our faith is a little foreign to us Catholics. But I also know of the great joy that we can feel when we talk about our faith honestly, sharing our joys and struggles with someone who is of like mind.

A great example of this faith-sharing is the Alpha Course. Many of those who participated in the ten-week journey have been Christian all their lives but never had an opportunity to talk about their Christian faith in a meaningful way. For many of them, the Alpha journey has changed their entire view of life as Christians and they are alive in the Spirit of Christ. This is the joy of sharing our faith with other believers.

Another example of faith-sharing is when we have our children baptised Catholic. However, the danger is that we often stop talking about our faith with the sacraments. Instead the sacraments are doors to the sacred and we are called to explore into and move beyond those sacraments into the mystery of Christ himself.

I believe one way to explore our faith is to share it with others of like mind. Maybe there is someone close to us with whom we have never taken the opportunity to start a conversation about faith. Or maybe we have someone who we already share with. 'Go now' and 'take nothing with you' and this week may we find someone with whom to share the experience of faith. Maybe that someone is very close such as our spouse or old friend or close family member. Or maybe it is a person at work or in the neighbourhood to whom you have not talked much. This week may we hear the urgency with which Jesus gives the church its mission and find someone to share our faith with. Like hiking in the Grand Canyon, may we never journey alone.

Fifteenth Sunday in Ordinary Time:
Deut 30:10-14; Col 1:15-20; Lk 10:25-37

Not Remaining at a Safe Distance

Recently I turned on the television to relax for a few minutes and I was quickly entranced by one of these so-called 'reality shows' called *Paradise Hotel*. I was intrigued by the Irish accent of the host who narrated us through a labyrinth of rules and regulations of the 'paradise hotel of love' where men and women room together to find out if they love one another. Each week they switch partners and someone gets eliminated!

I am not going to make any comment on the morality of the show or the shallowness of the 'love'. However, I was struck by how many people watch this show regularly. There are millions tuned in each week!

Love has become a 'spectator sport'.[1] It seems that we are quite comfortable watching others at 'love' and dream about love from a safe distant. We do not get involved because we might get hurt. Instead it is safer to watch and look at others! We remain at a safe distance and risk little or nothing. Another way to keep our distance from others is to intellectualise endlessly about love and the process.

The lawyer in today's gospel asks Jesus for more information about how to reach everlasting life. He knows the law of the Old Testament and in response to Jesus' rhetorical question he quotes the law exactly: 'Love the Lord your God with all your heart, with all your soul, with all your strength and with all your mind and your neighbour as yourself.' But the lawyer does not seem to understand the depth of the law. Jesus is unequivocal in his advice on application of the law and offers the parable of the Good Samaritan to illustrate his point of who is our neighbour.

In this story Jesus demonstrates that our actions show others who we really are. The actions of the priest and the Levite are not evil. The priest and Levite show the wounded man no malice or ill-will. Instead they just show complete indifference. Rather than be disturbed by contact with him they walk on the other side of the street. They remain at a safe distance and do not get involved. Jesus illustrates that by doing nothing we can sometimes do a great deal of wrong. By remaining at a 'safe distance' we can sin and at the very least we lose the opportunity to do good.

Yes, we are called to live the commandments as stated by the lawyer – to love God with all our hearts, souls, minds and all our strength. But we must apply these laws to everyone we come in contact with. We are called *not* to remain at a safe distance but instead become involved in people's lives. I suspect that many of us shy away from being involved in other's lives. We justify our behaviour like the priest and Levite by saying that we are 'minding our own business', or 'not judging someone else', or 'just letting others live their lives the way they want to.' The reality is that many of us see others who are struggling with life and we are called to get involved in a helping and loving manner.

Maybe it is someone who has lost a job and lost hope, or maybe it is a lonely neighbour or maybe it is someone in our own family who is in a destructive pattern of life, screaming for help in their own way. Whatever the scenario and whoever the person involved, we are called to resist the temptation of today's world, watching others at a safe distance. We are called to act like the Good Samaritan and get involved in loving our neighbour. We are called *not* to remain at a safe distance.

1. Inspired by this phrase used by William F. Maestri, *Grace Upon Grace*, (Makati, Philippines: St Paul Publications, 1988) 285.

Service Given, Gift Received

A man attending a crowded Mass refused to take off his hat when asked to do so by the ushers. Others also asked him to take off his hat, but he remained obstinate. The priest was most disturbed by his apparent lack of respect, and waited for him after Mass. He told the man that the community welcomes him as a guest and encourages him to join the parish. However, the priest explained they had a custom regarding men's hats and that in the future he hoped that he would conform. 'Thank you,' said the man. 'And thank you for taking the time to talk with me. It's good of you to invite me to join the community. Actually I joined the parish three years ago and have been coming regularly ever since, but today is the first time that anyone has ever paid any attention to me. After being unknown for three years, today, by simply keeping my hat on, I have had the pleasure of talking with the ushers, and now I have had a conversation with you, who always appeared too busy to talk to me before.'[1]

I hope that never happens to you at our church but I suspect that they are many people whom we fail to greet regularly. It is not just at church that people feel unwelcome, but also at work or at school or other places. Even in our own homes we may feel unwelcome, as if we disturb some unspoken rules of false harmony.

It seems that we have become so busy that we have no time to give quality attention to our children, our co-workers, co-students, not to mention the strangers among us. It seems that the only time we notice some people is when they act out of place or outside the customary behaviour. When they go against the grain, so to speak then we give them our 'negative' attention.

I think this is most true with our own children. When they don't get grades we come down on them or when they don't do something, then we notice them. It is also true of our friends and co-workers; we notice them only when they 'fail' to do something for us.

What would it take to convert that 'negative' attention to 'positive' attention? In today's gospel, Jesus visits two sisters, Mary and Martha and is welcomed by both of them in different ways. Mary sits at Jesus' feet and listens intently to his every word. She gives to him every ounce of her attention. Meanwhile Martha serves him with food and drink, and grumbles that Mary is not helping her serve. Jesus makes it very clear that Mary has chosen the greater part. Jesus says that the 'one thing necessary' for hospitality is attention to our guest, rather than some domestic performance.[2] If the guest is a prophet, the appropriate reception is listening to God's word. Jesus turns the point from one of providing a service to receiving a gift of grace.

Thus if we have someone visit us, the appropriate response is to give full attention to them and listen to our guest. In return we will receive a grace greater than our gift of our service.

Is this not true when we play with our children, giving them complete attention? We become surprised by some small action or word, and we can delight in its simple beauty.

Or when we genuinely listen to someone at the office or even at home and we discover something new about that person. Many of you married couples among us, despite the many years of living together, have discovered something new about your spouse through a conversation with a third party and you say, 'I never knew that, honey.'

Opening ourselves to genuine hospitality is not easy, because it requires full attention to others. We have to step outside ourselves. This week, may we notice the new parishioners among us, and the old parishioners whom we never knew. May we be open to each other, and be ready to serve one another by listening to each other's stories. May we notice the stranger at work or at school, and be ready to listen. May we notice the friend who sits beside us, and not wait till they fail us in some way. Today may we serve one another by our listening, and so receive the gift of grace in return.

1. Brian Cavanaugh, *The Sower's Seeds*, (Mahwah, New Jersey: Paulist Press, 1990) #85.
2. Luke Timothy Johnson, *The Gospel of Luke* (Sacra Pagina, Vol 3).

Put God First

Stephen Covey in his best selling book, *Seven Habits of Highly Effective Families*, shared a story of how a professor illustrated to his new class the need to prioritise their tasks for the semester. He brought in a large bowl half full of sand, a second large bowl half full of pebbles, a third large bowl almost full of large stones, as well as a jug full of water. He then challenged the class to fit all of these into one bowl. The class members protested that it was not possible, because all three bowls were almost full already not to mention the jug of water. One member insisted he had the answer, and he put the large stones on top of the pebbles, but there was not enough room for even the large stones and he failed. After much ado the professor showed them how it could be done. He took the bowl full of large stones and placed them in the centre, saying these large stones represent the most important and urgent tasks, so we put them first. Then he took the half-full bowl of pebbles, and poured them into the bowl full of large stones shaking it gently to allow all the pebbles to fall between the stones, explaining how these pebbles represented the important, but not urgent items. All the pebbles fit into the bowl as they moved into the gaps between the large stones. Then he took the sand and poured it on top, again shaking the bowl gently, allowing all the sand to fill all the crevices between the pebbles and the large stones. He explained that the sand represents those items that are not important, but often need to get done. Then he took the jug of water and poured it gently into the bowl and again it fitted into the bowl, filling it to the brim. This represents the many other things that need to get done but fit in between those things that are most important. How powerful an illustration that is for our lives![1]

Unfortunately, rarely do we follow the professor's advice, and we let the urgent, not important items fill our days. Sometimes, the non-urgent and non-important things fill our days, and we seem to get very little accomplished. Sometimes, we fill our day with mindless entertainment through television or idle conversation about other people's lives, and then we wonder where did the day go? Sometimes, we spend endless hours watching sports and then claim to have no time for family.

Sometimes we spend lots of time with our hobbies, and then claim to have no time for prayer.

What are our priorities, and how do we maintain them when the pressure comes to demand more in another area? I know that, in one sense, I am preaching to the choir as you are all here at Sunday Mass, but do we always make it here or do we always make time for our daily prayer?

I find myself constantly fighting for my prayer time. Whether it be against sleep or recreation, there is always competition for that prayer time. It seems to be always under attack.

In today's gospel, we are instructed on the Lord's Prayer, and we are told not only to pray, but we are told how to pray. Jesus invites us to always put God first even in our prayer, 'hallowed be thy name'. He strongly tells us that we are to put God's purposes first, 'thy kingdom come', and then go onto our own needs. This is the cornerstone of all prayer in my experience. To let God be first in our prayer, to thank him for the many gifts or challenges that day, to ask for his wisdom for the coming day, to allow his will to be done in our lives. Like the professor showing his students how to prioritise, so too was Jesus showing his disciples how to prioritise. He said to pray first before all else, and in our prayer to ask for God's will to be done through us and in us. We are called to do the same.

May we pray first before all else, and seek to make his will to be done in our lives. May we put God first this week for ourselves and our children.

---

1. Stephen R. Covey, *The Seven Habits of Highly Effective Families*, (New York: Golden Books, 1997) 160-161.

Share not Store

Several years ago friends of mine bought a house. It was a beautiful home with a delightful garden. Then they had some hardwood floors put down and they bought lovely new furniture to fill the house, including some new leather sofas. They decided to protect the hardwood floor by covering it with carpet and the new leather sofas by covering them with fabric.

Well I remember visiting them one night and as I entered their home I was asked to remove my shoes to protect the carpet. I know this is a custom in some cultures but this was for the furniture, not out of cultural reverence. I must admit I was afraid to sit on the sofa for fear they might ask me to remove my pants!

Later that evening we had a conversation about their need to protect their new house and furniture from usage. I asked them why bother get beautiful hardwood floors if we can never see them or soft leather sofas if we can never feel or see the leather. After little more discussion they agreed they had gone too far and later that month they removed some of their coverings.

Do we go too far in protecting or saving our possessions for another day – the proverbial rainy day? Or do we go too far in saving our possessions from use? Or, as the gospel says today, gathering things up in the storeroom of life?

We hear Jesus tell two brothers arguing over an inheritance that they have missed the point about life – they are being greedy. To illustrate his point he tells us a parable in which a man stores up his wealth so he can enjoy all of it later in life. Ironically that very night he will lose his life and never see his stored treasures again. Jesus is telling these two would-be disciples and us that we ought not to focus on storing but on sharing. He warns us against holding onto everything for ourselves. He calls us to share not store our treasures. So how do we share and what do we share?

It is my firm conviction that if we share what we have it will come back to us multiplied. If we give away things we generally receive much more in return. That is my real life experience that I testify to. Now, I do not mean that if I give my car away, I get back three cars in return. I think we would all gladly give away our cars then! I mean that when we give away something or give of ourselves we receive much more in return. For example, I give you the people of this parish my time and energy and I receive back so much love and generosity it is amazing. But more, the time and energy is multiplied because so many of you give of your time and energy. What is shared is multiplied.

The challenge then is to use what things we have and share them with others. Maybe it is rolling up the carpet and using the hardwood floors. Or folding the plastic or fabric of the sofas, so we and others can enjoy the beauty of lovely furniture. Or maybe it is to use the Waterford crystal we have collected. Or not to mind your new car getting dirty.

I mean to share wisely – let's not use our Waterford crystal with our children. But, why not use it with our friends or family? Whatever it is, we are called to share not store what we have. Most importantly we are called to share our very selves. We are invited to share everything we have with our family, our friends, and our neighbours. This is how we love – we share, not store.

Time is a Treasure

Several weeks ago I was watching the news on television and the reporter was giving some breaking news. A house had completely burned and he was now interviewing the family. 'How does it feel now that you have lost everything, your house, your car, everything you have ever owned?' inquired the reporter waiting for that news bit that will get him recognition. 'Wonderful,' exclaimed the woman while smiling brightly. The reporter stuttered for a moment, 'What – wonderful! Why?' 'I feel wonderful because I have my husband, my two children and, as a result of this, my neighbours are being extraordinarily generous, giving us food, shelter, and love. Everything else are just things!' as she smiled brightly into the camera. The reporter, still stunned by the answer, concluded his report somewhat disappointingly, 'There you have it, a family loses everything in a fire and they feel wonderful!'

The reporter felt, I am sure, that his report was a failure because it did not bring that 'disaster' news he was hoping. But I felt that it was a great report because that woman has her priorities right and she proclaimed it brilliantly. She is the living action of the today's gospel. 'Where your treasure is, there will your heart be.'

What are our treasures? What will we be remembered for when our time comes? In today's gospel we hear Jesus tell his disciples and us that in those things that we treasure will be where our hearts lie. Later in the gospel we also hear that we will be judged on how we use our treasures. We also know from other scripture that we are given different talents but we will be measured equally on how we put them to use.

However, I think one treasure that we are all given equally is time. Time is a God-given treasure. If you find that hard to believe ask someone who has been diagnosed with cancer. Or ask a person who has lost a loved one suddenly. Or ask yourself, do I have enough time for everything I want to do?

Well this treasure is given equally to all. Whether we are rich or poor, smart or not-so-smart, white, black, brown, or yellow, we all have the same amount of time each day. We all get 24 hours to spend each day. Not a second more or a second less. We may not have tomorrow but today we know we have! How do we spend that time? Do we have our priorities in order like the woman who lost her home and as Jesus invites us to have them – ordered to the kingdom of God?

In other words, do we spend our treasure-time for others? I know we live in a very busy world and time really is a commodity we wish we could trade in. However, we all get the same amount of time and we can evaluate how we use that time. I admit for myself I do not always use time well. Maybe you are the same.

Jesus calls us to use our treasures for the kingdom. We are invited to share our time with others. This week maybe we can find time for God in prayer. Or maybe we can spend some quality time with family. Maybe we can give some of our time to others who are squeezed for their time, like single parents.

This week we can use our treasure of time for God's kingdom and share it with others.

No Pain, No Gain

I recently watched television late at night, really late. Have you ever seen advertisements that late? Trust me, they are quite something. I am convinced that the quality is inversely proportional to the time of night. In other words, they get worse as the night goes on, figuring you and I are too tired to care. In any case, I saw the advertisement for one of the infamous exercise machines. I have forgotten the name now, bo-flex, solitaire, abducer, whatever the names! Yes, those machines modeled by people who never actually use them nor would they ever need to with their bodies. The advertisers lure us by the models and we are led to believe that we too can have bodies like them, if we buy these machines. Using the machines seems to be a secondary point. How to store these machines is always a selling point, sometimes it is only thing we do with them! Who among us does not have exercise machines at home collecting dust?

The reality is, using an old sports cliché, 'no pain, no gain'. Unless you really work out on these machines nothing is going to change any time soon. One has to be prepared to exercise to get stronger. It is the same when it comes to spiritual strength – no pain, no gain. Or put in religious terms – no cross, no glory.

In today's gospel Jesus is trying to inform his disciples about the realistic view of following him. He tells them that there is a cost of discipleship. He had come to kindle fire, to experience his baptism of suffering and death, and to cause a crisis of decision that led to dividing or even severing of the closest of bonds including family bonds.[1] Those who choose to follow him would then have to also share in the same cost, in the fire, the baptism, and the crisis of decision and division. The fire and baptism symbolise his pending death in Jerusalem and the division is that of the need to separate from the comforts of this world.

Jesus is giving the disciples, and us, the hard language today. We are challenged to stretch our spiritual muscles and feel the pain of exercise. We know if we do not push ourselves spiritually we will not get the growth and gain. Jesus leaves us under no illusion that this life of discipleship is passive. And if we live it to the fullest, according to his example, then there will be a cost.

The cost can be painful at times but it will always have its glory. We are challenged to really live the gospel values in our lives. What in our lives is contrary to the way of discipleship? How can we better live the gospel? What are the excess pounds that we need to shed so that we are spiritually stronger? Maybe it is greed. We want too much and hold on to too many things. Possessions can be overwhelming. Or maybe it is selfishness. We want to hold on to ourselves and not share our time or talents. Or maybe it is a lack of enthusiasm for the faith. We do not mention or talk about our beliefs to anyone. We keep all things to our selves. We are called to live for others and not for ourselves.

Whatever the excess pounds we have, and we all have different ones, Jesus, in today's gospel, is quite clear. We are called to realise the cost of discipleship. We are called to follow in his footsteps which will give us pain at times. Yet there is much to be gained because we will become spiritually stronger. This week, we can exercise our spiritual muscles and realise that there is no glory without the cross and no cross without the glory. This week we can take up some new habits like spending a few moments in prayer alone with God, doing some kind deeds for others, sharing our resources with others who have less, being enthusiastic about the faith we hold so dear and sharing our faith story with family or friends.

This week we can accept the reality of the gospel life and exercise our spiritual muscle and say no pain, no gain!

---

1. *Celebration: An Ecumenical Worship Resource,* (Kansas City, MO: National Catholic Reporter Company, Inc., August, 2001).

Being a Sacrament of Christ

Several years ago I had the opportunity to visit the Holy Land. One of the most venerated sites there is Christ's place of birth, Bethlehem. People come from all corners of the earth to Manger Square where the large Church of the Nativity is located.[1] While the church is large and imposing, the door is short and narrow. For someone my size, believe me when I say it is a challenge to fit through. However, that is the only entrance into the church. If one wants to get in one has to pass through the narrow gate. When inside, to get to the location of the birthplace of Christ, one has to descend a narrow, steep staircase. And you know what is at the bottom of the staircase? Yes. Another door, and yes, the door is short and narrow. In order to reach the place of pilgrimage one must be willing to humbly stoop low through the doorway and rise up one's feet high to get over the threshold, through the narrow and short door.

How appropriate that image is for reaching the birthplace of Christ. To follow Christ we ought to be humble and courageous. Humble to know we need to bend our will to his. Courageous to pick ourselves up when we fall.

This image is helpful when listening to today's gospel. Jesus talks about the narrow gate of salvation. Most biblical scholars agree that the narrow gate to which Jesus is referring is himself. Christ is the narrow gate of salvation. Christ is the way, the truth, and the life. He says that whoever comes to him will have new life. S/he who knows him knows the Father. Christ is the resurrection and the life. In Christ we move and live and have our being. So we need to live in and through Christ to have new life. Christ is the centre to which our lives ought to be focused. So we ought to live in and through Christ. We are called to live as Christ lived. We are called to *be* Christ.

This is what the church teaches. It was re-affirmed at the Second Vatican Council, when they acknowledged that Christ is the primordial sacrament. Christ is the sacrament from which all others take their meaning. When we are baptised we are baptised into Christ. We have new life in and through Christ. We put on the clothes of Christ. When we receive First Communion, and indeed every time we receive eucharist at this table each Sunday, we receive the Body and Blood of Christ. When we get confirmed we affirm our belief that Christ Jesus is the Saviour of the World and we promise to follow him. When we partake in the sacraments of healing – reconciliation and anointing – we are healed in and through the touch of Christ. We are reconciled with God through the power of Christ and we are anointed in the name of Christ. Then in the sacraments of commitment or discipleship we are brought into Christ even more. In the sacrament of Holy Orders I and others are ordained to love by serving as Christ did – *in persona Christi*. And in the sacrament of Matrimony, in which many of you have participated, you commit to love one another in the same way Christ loves his church.

So you see, all the sacraments are based in Christ. They only make sense in and through Christ. Remember they symbolise and *are* what they symbolise. For example, the bread and wine symbolise and are the Body and Blood of Christ. The same ought to be said of us as Christians. We ought to be a sacrament of Christ. So we ought to be the first ones to let the waters of baptism wash away our sins and those of others. We ought to not only receive the Body of Christ here, but we ought to become the bread of life to others, nourishing their weakened faith outside of here. We ought to be the first to confirm and affirm our faith in Christ and be proud to proclaim we believe, whenever we get a chance. We ought to be the first to reconcile and to be reconciled with, holding no grudges. We ought to be the first to give the healing power of touch to those who are sick and in need of healing. And we ought to be the first to commit our lives to Christ in love whether for one person or many.

Today the gospel reminds us that we are called to live in and through the narrow gate – Christ Jesus. We are all invited to eternal life but we need to accept the invitation.

This week maybe we can not only symbolise what Christ has done for us but also *be* Christ to others. Let us walk through the narrow gate of Christ and become the sacrament of Christ to others.

Twenty-second Sunday in Ordinary Time:

---

1. Inspired by a story given by Patricia Datchuck Sanchez in *Celebration: An Ecumenical Worship Resource*, (Kansas City, MO: National Catholic Reporter Company, Inc., August, 2001).

All are Invited to the Heavenly Banquet

Last week I received this formal wedding invitation in the mail and it reads,

> *Rev Brendan McGuire, you are cordially invited*
> *to the wedding banquet of Peter and Barbara ...*

Even though as a priest I am regularly receiving wedding invitations, it is always nice to receive the formal invitation. Especially when it reads so eloquently – one feels so important, if only for a few minutes!

Do you remember when you were invited to something formal? Was it a wedding, or baby shower, or graduation or someone's birthday party or maybe a something formal at work or house blessing party? Whatever it was it makes us feel good when we read those words ...

> *You are cordially invited to ...*

Sometimes when we find out who else got invited we can be disappointed. We might think, 'Why did she or he get invited?' Somehow we think our invitation is lessened because of the number of others. I was once at a wedding where there were 1000+ guests – I think they invited everyone they ever met! When I got there I thought, 'Everyone is here!' Another example was when I got invited to be in a top executive book and I thought how special I was. Then I found out that there were over 4000 other people also invited.

Sometimes we can think if we are not the only ones, then we are not special. Well Christ Jesus has sent everyone here present an invitation to his heavenly banquet. Yes, we are all invited. Indeed all people everywhere are invited. However, we have to accept the invitation. And when we accept the invitation we ought not to complain about who else got invited. It is a joy to which all people are called. In other words, we ought to be humble about our invitation, knowing that we did not deserve it. So after we accept, then what?

Just like when we go to a wedding banquet, we prepare. For this banquet it is a lifetime of preparation. So how do we prepare? In today's gospel we hear Jesus give us some advice. At first look we might think that Jesus is giving us guidance about dinner etiquette, who should sit where and how to get honour at table. But there is much more to this than that surface reading. Jesus is a little more than the male version of Miss Manners. No! Jesus gives us the preparation recipe for life.

We are called to be humble in everything we do and say. Before I go any further I need to distinguish between false humility and authentic humility. False humility is the self-abasing type – 'Oh I am not worthy … I have no value … I have no gifts!' *Wrong!* We all have value and we all have gifts. It is false humility to deny oneself. On the other hand, authentic humility is recognising that one has gifts and we are called to use them for the good of others. Authentic humility says that I do not judge others because I know I am weak too. Yes, we are all sinners but we are all called to the table.

So we are called to listen to the invitation from Christ and accept it. Then we are called to prepare by recognising our gifts and using them for the good of others. Are there gifts I have that I do not share with others? Music, paintings, poetry, teaching, visiting the sick, serving the homeless or caring for our relatives. Whatever it is, this week we can accept the invitation to the Lord's heavenly banquet by preparing for it in humble service of others.

Loving till it Hurts

When I was growing up in Ireland, I was regularly reminded of the importance of family. 'Blood is thicker than water' was a common expression.[1] I am sure you have heard it. I think the theme is common in nearly every culture in every country in the world – to defend the family unit no matter what. I know that it is true of Irish and Italians. I know that it is true of Vietnamese and Filipinos. I know it is true for Hispanics. And I know it is true even in the US where individuality is held high.

But in today's gospel we hear Jesus say, 'Hate your father and mother, hate your wife and children, your brother and sister and even your very self' in order to follow him as a disciple. What are we to make of this? Are we really to hate instead of love?

Well, we need to understand who wrote this passage and the context in which it was written. Firstly, this is St Luke's gospel and it is the section called 'call to discipleship', where Luke warns potential followers of Jesus about the cost of discipleship. Secondly, the word used in the Greek 'to hate' does not have the same meaning as we use it today. It is more a 'putting into second place' or 'turning away from'. It is a way of speaking that puts emphasis on one thing over another. In other words, Jesus is saying that we ought not to prioritise over God.

Put simply, we are called to love God with all our hearts, all our minds, and all our souls. And we are called to love our neighbour as ourselves. Yes, we are called to love above everything else. We are called to love no matter what. We are called to love until it hurts and then some. So maybe Jesus would change the phrase and say, 'Blood is not thicker than baptismal water', or 'We are all in the same family'.

We are all called to love one another no matter what. Now I do not mean we are called to remain in dysfunctional or abusive relationships. Sometimes we might need to love by leaving those relationships. No, I am talking about loving those who are difficult to love. Love those people in our lives who seem not to love themselves anymore. Those people who seem to have given up on life itself. Often that is someone very close. It is sometimes harder to love someone closer to us. Maybe it is our spouse who was unfaithful. Maybe it is our child who has strayed from life and is abusing drugs. Maybe it is our parent who seems distant and cannot relate to us. Maybe it is someone at work who did not get laid off while we did. Maybe it is our spouse of many years and the spark is gone from our marriage. Maybe it is a friend who has lost all hope.

Yes, we are called to love these people because we *are* God's love to them. We are called to not give up on them. We are called to love them until it hurts. We are to love them even more because they have no one else.

Who in our lives needs our love? Who in our lives needs to feel God's love through us? This week we can make the baptismal water thicker than blood by loving till it hurts.

Who is that person?

---

1. Adapted from idea given in Jude Siciliano, OP, *Preachers Exchange*, (Raleigh, NC: preachex@opsouth.org).

Twenty-fourth Sunday in Ordinary Time:
Ex 32:7-11, 13-14; 1 Tim 1:12-17; Lk 15:1-32

Forgive – Practice First!

That gospel passage today is the scripture assigned for today, the 24th Sunday of Ordinary Time. We have heard those parables often over the years especially the parable of the prodigal son. But how different they sound today! Oh how different they sound in the context of Tuesday's terrorist attacks in the East Coast. Oh how difficult they are to hear today!

So how are we to make sense of them today? What is the Lord trying to tell us? This week I went to get my haircut. After I sat down my barber started cutting and then suddenly he stopped, with the scissors in one hand and the shears in the other hand. He asks, 'Father, I have a professional question.' I thought to myself, 'I just want a haircut!' But I knew in light of the events of Tuesday a tough question was coming. And so he proceeded, 'I was listening to the radio today and some preacher told us that we must forgive the perpetrators of the terrorist attacks in New York and Washington. The question I have for you, Father, is *how?* How can we possibly forgive such hideous and cowardly acts? How can we forgive such terror?'

One word came to my mind – practice. Yes, practice! I mean we cannot expect to forgive these terrorists who have perpetrated these horrendous acts if we have no practice in forgiving. In other words, we need to practice forgiveness first. Forgiving our family and friends maybe! What hope do we have of forgiving the terrorists if we have never forgiven anybody close to us before. I am not suggesting that forgiving is easy. On the contrary, I know from firsthand experience it is very difficult. It is a process that takes time. Anyone who has been betrayed by a friend or family member knows that the pain is immense. Or the pain of hurtful comments from one group or other. Or the pain of lies and false accusations. No, anyone who knows pain knows that forgiveness doesn't come easily. It is a process that takes time and yet God always calls us to forgive.

In today's scripture we hear Jesus tell us three parables of forgiveness, the lost sheep, the lost coin, and the most poignant, the prodigal son. Each of these tells us of God's care and love for us. God will search for us even though we are lost. God will celebrate if even one of us turns away from sin and back to him. Most vividly in the story of the prodigal son, we hear of God's immense and boundless love. He welcomes back a strayed son after a long exile. He wants to welcome back every sinner into his arms. God does not forgive us because we are worthy of forgiveness. Nor do we forgive others because they are worthy of forgiveness. On the contrary, we are forgiven despite our unworthiness. And on the contrary, we forgive despite their unworthiness. We forgive because we have been forgiven by God first.

It is never easy to forgive and most of us know that. So where do we start? We need to first understand what forgiveness is and what forgiveness is not. Forgiving is not forgetting. I do not think there is a person in this church, in the United States of America, or, dare I say it, in the world who will forget September 11, 2001. It will be forever etched into our minds as a day of terror and pointless violence. No, forgiving is not forgetting nor should it be. Forgiving is not revenge or retaliation. For then we would be no better off than the perpetrators of these cowardly acts. Instead, forgiveness is seeking justice at all times. And justice is based in truth. And the truth is that there is only a remote chance that a terrorist lives in our community. And if they did we would never really know for the nature of a terrorist is to be secret and hidden. And justice is sought by those who are empowered to bring it about. There are agencies in our country that will seek and find the truth.

Once we have truth then we can seek justice. We are not charged to bring these people to justice but there are those whose responsibility it is. So we have no right to hold any person, or group of people, or creed of people in our community accountable for the actions of others. They did not do those acts of terrorism. Justice will be found when the truth is revealed to us in time. Instead, forgiveness starts in our own community. Forgiveness starts with you and me forgiving each other the wrongs we do. If we can practice that first, then we will bring defeat to those people of hate. If we can forgive our spouses for their lack of fidelity or breakdown in their love, or our children who they have drifted away from us, or our parents who don't seem to understand us, or our friends who have betrayed us in some way, or our neighbours who are not friendly to us.

If we can do this then we change these actions of hatred into actions and words of love and forgiveness.

Please, I implore you this week or in the weeks ahead, do not succumb to the temptation to hate in return. Do not succumb to the temptation to demand retaliation or vengeance. Instead let us take victory over hatred and love those close to us by forgiving them the hurt they have inflicted on us.

Let us not serve the perpetrators of these hideous crimes a victory; instead, let us win by loving our neighbours even more. Please, I beg you – forgive.

We can practice with our family, friends, and neighbours. This week we can take victory by practising forgiveness and love. As our closing song says,

'Let there be peace on earth and let it begin with me!'

This homily was given the Sunday following September 11th terrorist attacks in New York City, 2001.

Priority of Prayer

There is a story told of two boys who found a purse in a parking lot. When the boys opened the purse it contained the lady's name and a ten-dollar bill. One of the boys said to the other, 'It probably belongs to that little old lady who went out before us.' The other boy immediately replied, 'We cannot keep it, we'll have give it back.' And then added, 'But let's change the ten-dollar bill into ten ones. So she can give us a decent tip for finding her purse.' Smart kids, ohh!

Many of us know that waiters/waitresses will do the same when they return our change in restaurants. Even kids can be smart enough to know how to make a buck or two. Smart in world ways!

In today's gospel we hear Jesus praise the dishonest steward, not for his dishonesty, but for his shrewdness. This dishonest steward knows well enough to look after himself when it comes to worldly possessions. Jesus then pleads with his listeners, if we can be that wise with worldly things then we ought to be as wise in heavenly matters. He asks us to set our priority on God and our journey back to him.

However, we often get so caught up with worldly things that our relationship with God takes a distant second place. How do we set our priority on God? Since September 11th I have heard from different people how their lives have changed. I think that is true of us all. Who on September 11th, upon hearing of the terrorist attacks, did not call loved ones to check and see if they were okay? I believe most people that day went home early and spent quality time with family and friends. And rightly so!

When it comes to major disasters we quickly reset our priorities. On September 10th it was illegal to pray in school. On September 11th I do not think there was a school in the country whose teachers did not pray with their children.

That is resetting priorities to where they ought to be. Maybe we can make permanent those changes in our lives since the September 11th terrorist attacks. I mean making a priority of family and friends. Make a priority of praying to God always.

In today's second reading from Paul's first letter to Timothy we hear the words in the context of the world events. It is serendipitous that these words occur this Sunday. Paul exhorts Timothy to pray for kings and those in authority that they may lead us in peaceful lives. He says we ought to pray for them with grateful hearts, free from anger. After the President's speech the other night we are all no doubt aware that we are on the brink of war with an invisible and lethal enemy. Yes, our leaders need our prayers. I do not mean need as in want. No, I mean *need* as in necessity. They need our prayers so that they make wise decisions, seeking justice and truth and not revenge and retaliation.

We are called this week to make prayer a priority. Pray for those who lead our nation. This week maybe we can be wise in heavenly matters and pray.

Let us promise each other today to make it a priority to pray this week. To cut time out every single day this week and pray for our president and all nations' leaders that they may act wisely and justly in all matters. Pray that they may seek the truth and justice and not seek revenge or retaliation. Pray that they seek guidance from the Holy Spirit in all matters.

Also let us pray for one another that we do not succumb to hatred in our own lives. Instead, pray that we overcome the hatred of these hideous crimes against our people. Pray that we can love and forgive. Pray that we can treat all people with dignity and love.

This week may we pray for one another and I implore you to hold our leaders in our prayers.

Make it a priority to pray this week.

What We Fail to Do!

Several years ago, when I was living in Sunnyvale not far from here, we had a storm come through and it blew down the fence between our neighbours and ourselves. Do you know that was the first time I met our neighbours! I lived there for at least two years and I never once introduced myself nor did they. I was told that is not done here. 'Leave them be,' I was told. Ironically, in the process of building back the fence, that wall separating us, we got to know each other and became friends. Strange, isn't it, that we need such an event to realise who lives next door!

Do you know your neighbours? In California we are known for our 'live and let live' attitude. We don't interfere with each other's business. We have our differences but we respect each other and let others do their thing as long we can do our thing. We are liberal and trusting of one another. 'Live and let live' is the attitude.[1]

However, in another context, such an attitude could be perceived as a 'Live and let die' attitude. Our so-called let live attitude could also be understood to be an attitude of indifference, a desire *not* to be involved. We see some friends destroy their lives and we stay away rather than be seen to meddle in others' private matters. We see abuses of people's rights at work or ethnic groups and we say nothing for fear that something will happen to us. We see our families fracture over some misunderstanding and we stand by for fear of being labelled trouble-maker. So our 'live and let live' attitude can have some negative consequences.

In today's gospel we hear about an anonymous rich man and a poor man named Lazarus. We should know where this story is going when we hear that the rich man has no name and the poor man has a name. The Jesus of the gospel of Luke always favours the poor man. The rich man is condemned by God not for what he did but what he *failed* to do. He was not condemned because he was rich, but because he failed to use his wealth appropriately. He was not condemned for having too much food but for not sharing it with others. He was not condemned for dressing well, but for not enabling others to be dressed at all. He was not condemned for what he did to Lazarus, but because of what he failed to do for him. The fact is that the rich man never noticed Lazarus at all. He walked past him every day and never saw him. He did not kick him or spit on him. He just ignored him. He was indifferent to his struggle for life. He effectively said, live and let live. Or in reality he said, live and let die.

Who in our lives do we walk past every day and not notice? It is probably not a homeless person. Most of us live in good neighbourhoods, where we have few or no homeless people *per se*. But there is more to a home than a house. We can be homeless in different ways. We can be homeless in the sense that we have no family or friends.

Who are the homeless in our lives? Maybe it is the reception-ist or secretary at work who we walk past every day and do not know their name. Or maybe it is the janitor or maintenance workers at school who we see every day but never greet them. Or maybe it is that person who sits alone at lunch and we never talk with them, because they look strange or talk funny. Who is the homeless, nameless person in our lives that we walk past every day?

This week let us promise each other that we will find in our lives just one person – just one – who is homeless or nameless and be Christ to them. That we will not be the rich man of today's parable but instead reach out to the Lazarus in our lives. Then next week when we come back here to the eucharist, we can say 'Yes we found someone and brought them the living Christ.'

Who is the Lazarus in our life that we need to stretch out to?

---

1. Adapted from William F. Maestri, *Grace Upon Grace*, (Makati, Philippines: St Paul Publications, 1988) 306.

Servant of the Lord

Many of you know that I am the youngest of twelve children. There were eight boys going to the same school every morning. You can imagine the bedlam setting off to school each day. One of things I always remember was the magnificent dinners my mother would have ready every day. You see in Ireland when I was growing up we had the main meal of the day at 1pm in the afternoon. I remember most especially the large saucepan of soup, almost the size of a bucket. A delicious hot soup on those wintry days was always welcome and we had a lot of those wintry days in Ireland! We would eat dinner and head back to school. Then, returning from school after rugby practice, we would come home and nearly always we would find mom sleeping in the sofa with a newspaper in her hands. I used to think, 'Ah, what a life! I can't wait till I finish school so I could do that.'

Then one day I was sick and got to stay at home. After a few days I was better and I could walk around the house and so I followed my mom around for the day. My view of my mom would never be the same! As soon as my brothers headed off to school she cleaned up after breakfast. Then immediately she prepared dinner, shopping and frantically cutting vegetables for the soup. It took hours to prepare those meals.

She never stopped from the moment my brothers left for school till they returned for their meal. Then they would saunter in, scoff down the food and disappear as fast as they arrived. Then my mom would clean up after them and she would be exhausted from the day's work. About 15 minutes before my brothers arrive in again she would sit by the fire and attempt to read the newspaper and inevitably fall asleep. Then my brothers arrived in and she got up and prepared evening tea for them.

That was my mother's routine for over thirty years and never once did she complain about her role as mother. You see to my mother she was just being 'mother' and nothing more. My mother served my brothers, sisters and me every waking day of her life as mother.

In a lot of ways that does not change although with old age

we are given the opportunity to return the service. I think most of us have someone in our lives like my mother. Maybe it is your mother or maybe it is your father. Maybe it is your grandmother or grandfather. Or maybe it is a close friend who you know to be that humble servant. Yes, most of us have someone who exemplifies humble service.

In today's gospel we hear Jesus tell his disciples about the servant who is called to serve and the analogy of faith to a mustard seed. The story of the servant might sounds harsh to us but Jesus is pointing out the obvious role that a servant plays. Namely, they are called and paid to serve. That is what is expected from them. And then he tells us that is what is expected of us! In other words, we are called to serve in our way. What is our way?

Like my mother we are called to be what we are to the fullest extent. We are not necessarily called to extraordinary acts although some of us are. Most of us are called to do our ordinary things in extraordinary ways. In other words we are called to do the actions of every day life with the extraordinary love and care that comes from God.

If we are mothers, then let us be mothers with love, passion, and compassion. If we are fathers, then let us be fathers with love, passion, and compassion. And if we are children, then we can recognise the gift of our parents. Today maybe we can pause for a moment and offer praise and thanksgiving to God for our parents who serve us every day of our lives. And maybe we can challenge ourselves to be a humble servant of God this week.

Maybe we can find a way to serve someone and not ask for praise, but instead do it in such a way that it becomes extraordinary.

Today, let us be servants of the Lord to one another.

Think, Thank, and Believe in God

Many of you have heard me talk of my niece and nephew who live nearby and how their lives are lessons to me. I was recently fascinated by my niece's speedy ability to learn. She now constructs full sentences and is able to understand conversations very well. One of the things she is learning is what to say at certain times. For example, when she asks for something she says, 'Please'. And when she receives something she says, 'Thank you'. But you know that is very much learned behaviour. It takes time to learn and is not instinctive, it seems. Parents often remind their children to say the words: 'Say thank you', 'What do you say?', 'Did you say thank you?' We all consider this a good thing for our children. Fundamentally it is good manners in dealing with others.

Well, today's gospel is *not* about good manners! Jesus is *not* saying that we need good manners. Although I am sure that Jesus would agree that polite behaviour and good manners between us is good. Jesus' message is about faith. Jesus is not waiting for the lepers to return and thank him as if he was a parent teaching manners. No! Instead Jesus asks the question of faith: 'Were not all ten healed? Did they not believe? ...Your faith has saved you.'

We can deduce from the scripture passage that nine of the lepers were Jews and one was a Samaritan. Only the Samaritan, the foreigner, came back to thank God for his healing. He did this after he thought about what had happened to him.

When Jesus said, 'Go and show yourselves to the priests,' he was asking them to obey the law which stated that only the priests could pronounce lepers clean. So they all believed enough to go and see the priests and only one realised the actual power of healing. Out of gratitude he goes back to Jesus and says thank you.

If we examine what happens here we see that the Samaritan first thinks about what happens and then he realises the gift he has received in faith. And his first action in faith is to be grateful.

We are called to follow the example of the Samaritan and think about our lives. Then out of realisation of the gifts we have received in faith, we turn to God in gratitude. So where do we start?

Richard Carlson in his book, *Don't Sweat the Small Stuff ... and it's all small stuff*, addresses the issue of ingratitude. He says that few of us remain ungrateful intentionally. Yet we often go from day to day being ungrateful. He suggests that we could spend a moment every day and think of just one person to be thankful for and then thank them. Not a bad idea for where we can start – thankfulness for one person!

Our faith tells us that God is ever-present in the world. In other words, God is always with us. If that it is the case then most of us miss him most of the time. If we cannot see him it is because we are blind to his presence. To see him we must train ourselves to think and reflect on our daily lives. One of the best places to start is gratitude. We can stop and think about today and ask, 'Who am I thankful for today?' And then thank God for that person and then thank that person too.

I believe we will act out of our faith! Then we can transform this table of wood in this place to a true table of thanksgiving where we genuinely offer our thanks to God.

Today, who is the one person for whom we can be thankful? Maybe we can bring that name to this table and offer praise and thanksgiving to God for them. Maybe it is our mother or father, who gives constantly to us. Maybe it is our spouse, who is the ever-present love in our lives. Maybe it is our children, despite their quirks; they give us so much joy. Or maybe it is that person at work or school, who helped us learn something new. Or maybe it is our friend who has always been there leading us to grow. Whoever it is today, we promise to be thankful for one person and bring them to the table of the Lord.

Then this week we can transform our good manners into a genuine statement of faith, and be thankful to God for someone each day. Today and every day we think, thank, and believe in God by thanking God for one person each day.

Pray Always Without Growing Weary

I was recently fascinated by the way we, as humans, develop our means to communicate. From infant to adult we communicate in very different ways. When we are infants, how do we communicate? Yes, we cry! Seriously, when we are infants the only means of communication is through our crying. We cry if we want food. We cry if we want our diaper changed. We cry if we want love. We cry if we are sick. And parents can tell the difference between the different cries!

Then we grow up a little and we learn words. We use our hands to point to things we want and say, 'juice,' 'milk,' 'bread,' etc. Then we get a few more words and express it differently: 'I want more juice,' 'I want more food now.' Then we get a little older still and we use full sentences with more understanding: 'I want new shoes, because these do not match my outfit,' 'I want a new bicycle, because Johnny has a new one.' We may not like what we hear, but they are communicating.

Then we become teenagers and we find out that to get what we want is more work, and so we do some work first. For example, I vacuum the house, clean the car, and then ask, 'Mom, can I go to a party with my friends on Friday night?' We get a little more manipulative in a naïve way. Then there is a stage where we feel we need to tell the whole truth, bluntly. We really do not care what others think. For example, 'I am not going to Mass anymore.' And we ask, 'Why is that?' 'Because I do not like it and it's boring!' Well, well let's not be bashful!

Then we develop into adults and we find that this communication is hard work. We realise that we need to listen more to understand and we find that others want to communicate too. Eventually as adults we realise that communication is a two-way street and requires a commitment to listen as well as talk. Anyone involved in any relationship realises that we are called to this commitment of honest communication.

In today's gospel we hear Jesus share with his disciples the necessity to pray always and without growing weary. We, too, are called to pray always. Prayer can be understood as communication with God in the same way as when we communicate with any friend or family member. Then we need to ask ourselves are we committed to that relationship when it comes to communication? Where are we at currently in our communication with God? Are we still infants crying when we want something? Or are we still a young child telling God what we want, I want this, and I want that? Or are we arguing with God about the way we see things, believing that we are completely right like teenagers? Or are we rebellious in our attitudes towards God? Or are we developing into adults and understanding that prayer is an honest two-way communication with God? Are we committed to our communication with God, knowing that it requires work on our behalf to listen?

We are all called to an adult prayer life, and we are invited to listen in our prayer to what God has to say. Where are we at in our prayer life and can we challenge ourselves to grow and pray always without growing weary?

Be Merciful to Me, a Sinner!

A few years ago I read a book called *The Spirituality of Imperfection*. It is wonderful book about the spirituality of the Alcoholics Anonymous (AA) – the support groups who usually meet weekly to comfort each other in their struggle against alcoholism. One of the points that touched me most while reading the book was the reason that Alcoholics Anonymous is considered a success. The book says that the success in the programme is the meetings and suggests the reason people return to every meeting is not their strength, but their weakness. The thing that always draws them together is the fact that they will never be able to drink alcohol – their weakness. People from all walks of life are afflicted by this disease – men and women, young and old, white collar and blue collar workers, every creed, every race, every type of person. They still come together because they know their common weakness. It levels the playing field for all to share equally.

I wonder if we could learn something from their 'spirituality of imperfection'. The thing that draws us together here every Sunday is that we know we are imperfect too. We are all sinners. There is a tax collector in all of us. Although we do not all have the same weakness. Indeed, we probably all have different weaknesses. We all know that we are sinful in some way. We are *not* perfect. If we think we have no sins then we have just sinned, the sin of pride!

Every Sunday we come to this table to be reconciled with God and with one another. At the beginning of Mass each week we pause to acknowledge our sinfulness. We come from different places, different spaces, and different families. We say, Lord have mercy, Christ have mercy, Lord have mercy. We acknowledge that we have sinned and we acknowledge we need God's mercy and love. But we can often sound like the Pharisee and pray that we are not like others who sin more than we do. Or we fly past that moment so quickly that we do not really enter into a self-reflection.

We are called to examine ourselves honestly and ask for true forgiveness out of authentic acknowledgement of our sins. None of us is perfect; we are all sinners in one way or another. That's why Jesus' words are a wake up call to us today, a call to reflection and a call to self-evaluation.

Later in the Mass we will say, 'I am not worthy to receive you but only say the word and I shall be healed.' We acknowledge our explicit need for God's forgiveness, but do we really mean it?

Today we come to this table to celebrate God's role in our lives, but first we pause and acknowledge just one way in which we are a sinner. Maybe we failed ourselves this week. Or maybe it was a family member we said or did something against. Or maybe it was a neighbour or friend we failed to do something for.

Let us pause again right now and think specifically of something and say 'Lord, I am a sinner.' Maybe we can do that same exercise of self-reflection each night before we fall asleep and ask God for mercy.

Maybe now we can go to the Lord at this table, and along with the tax collector, we can say, 'O God, be merciful to me a sinner!'

Hiding Place

One of my favorite poems is *The Hound of Heaven* by Francis Thompson.[1] Maybe you know it or have read it. It is a wonderful story of the human spirit. Francis Thompson, born in the nineteenth century, had a difficult life of poverty, failure, illness, and drug addiction which almost killed him. Then he was cared for by an elderly couple and he saw God in them. He ultimately found God late in his life. This poem describes how Thompson searched for God while at the same time he attempted to flee from God. In the end God was like the Hound of Heaven who always searched for him and God never gave up searching.

I love this poem because it seems to describe for me how I hid from God for so many years myself. I often refer to this poem when I talk about my vocation to leave the business world and become a priest. Not that I lived a life of poverty, illness, or drug addiction, but I genuinely tried to flee the Lord's call for many years.

I fled him, down the nights and down the days;
I fled him, down the arches of the years;
I fled him, down the labyrinthine ways
Of my own mind; and in the midst of tears
I hide from him, and under running laughter.
Up vistaed hopes I sped;
And shot, precipitated,
Adown Titanic glooms of chasmed fears,
From those strong feet that followed, followed after.
But with unhurrying chase,
And unperturbed pace,
Deliberate speed, majestic instancy,
They beat – a voice beat
More instant than the feet –
'All things that betray thee, who betrayest me.'

It is a beautiful poem about how we search for God while also fleeing from him.

And yet it is God who searches for us, who never gives up on us. No matter what we do or how far we drift God is always just an arm's stretch away. He is that hound of heaven who keeps on coming. In today's gospel we hear about Zaccheus who searches for Jesus. He is trying to see Jesus and find his way in life. We might think upon first hearing this gospel, the focus is Zaccheus' search for Jesus and his success therein. However, I believe that it is more about God searching for Zaccheus than Zaccheus searching for Jesus.

The last words of the gospel are the key to unlock its meaning, 'The Son of Man has come to seek and to save what was lost.' Zaccheus was lost. Zaccheus was a chief tax collector and a wealthy man from ill-gotten gains. He was hated and despised by his fellow Jews. Yet Jesus still searches for Zaccheus.

This is a powerful example of God's forgiving love at work in the ministry of Jesus.[2] Like Zaccheus, we search for God in all sorts of ways and places. We are all believing people otherwise we would not be here. Yet we know we have searched for God in our own lives and sometimes in the wrong places. Maybe we seek God in our success at our workplace, willing to do anything to move up the corporate ladder. Maybe we seek God in school to the point of cheating to get good grades. Maybe we seek God in looking good to the point of spending all our money on expensive clothes. Maybe we seek God in being a likeable neighbour to the point of ignoring the injustice of gossip and malice.

Whenever we are ready to turn back to God we will realise that God is as close to us as our shadow. He is as close to us as the air that we breathe. All we need to do is turn back. I am not talking about a partial turnaround, a glance back at God, but a total about turn! God wants us to realise that he is always there, ready to forgive and welcome us home.

Later in today's liturgy we will hear a song called *Hiding Place*.[3] Maybe we can reflect on our search for God and God's ever-present search for us as the hound of heaven. Maybe today and this week we can ask ourselves, what small part of our lives are we hiding from God?

1. Francis Thompson, 'Hound of Heaven' in *The Top 500 Poems*, ed. William Harmon (New York: Columbia University Press, 1992) 843.
2. William F. Maestri, *Grace Upon Grace*, (Makati, Philippines: St Paul Publications, 1988) 317.
3. Fr Liam Lawton, Diocese of Kildare and Leighlin, Ireland.

Life is Good and When You Die Life is Great!

My brother and his wife went to a seminar this week on how to parent better. The presenters were a married couple who are child psychologists and renowned authors. They have written several books on raising children, one on raising a boy, another on a girl, another on a teenager, etc. One of the things my brother took away from this lecture was a phrase that caught my attention: 'Life is difficult, and then you die.' Life is difficult and then you die! How depressing!

I understand they were trying to reassure parents that raising children is difficult and it is never easy, no matter how good the children are. Look for meaning in your life by making the best of it. We gain meaning from what we do and therefore do the best you can when raising your children.

Unfortunately this message leads to a problem – it does not harmonise with our faith. Our faith says that when we die there is more. We believe that Jesus lived among us, died, and rose from the dead. We believe in the resurrection. That is what we celebrate every Sunday when we come to this table. We will have life after death. We believe in more now and more later, after death that is. We believe that life is good and when we die it is great! Yes, life can be challenging, sometimes very challenging, especially if you are raising children. But we believe that we get meaning from who we *are* more than what we *do*. We are children of God and no matter what we do that does not change. For this reason we, as Christians, see things differently in life.

In today's gospel we hear about the Sadducees who ask Jesus what happens when we die?[1] It's a question that seems authentic at first reading. It is important, however, to remember that the Sadducees did not believe in the resurrection. Like our psychologist friends, they said that life is difficult and then you die. They ask the question of Jesus not to find an answer, but to trip Jesus up and find ways to discredit him. Nonetheless Jesus answers the question with piercing precision. We are all children of God and God is a living God who cares for the living and the dead. In other words, God loves us from beginning to eternity. So then the questions for us are: How do we live as people who believe in the resurrection? How do we live differently as Christians?

I do not want to suggest a Pollyannaish view of life where everything is wonderful and sweet with no real problems. No! I know life can be difficult at times. Sometimes it's extraordinarily difficult – like the loss of a loved one, the breakup of a friendship, the loss of a job which seems more common today. Yes, life can be difficult. But that is not the end nor is it the beginning. Difficult spots in our lives are somewhere in the middle. We will get past them as we have in the past. It is how we handle them that counts.

As Christians we believe we do not have to be alone in these difficult spots. We can get past them together, together in Christ. You see, we believe we have each other for these difficult spaces in our lives and that is our strength as a community of believers. But we need to ask for help and be willing to help if asked.

This week, as we go forth from here, we ought to ask ourselves if I am in a difficult spot, who can I reach out to? Maybe it is our parents or brother or sister. Maybe it is our children. Maybe it is our friends or teachers at school. And how do I ask for help?

On the other hand, if we are in a good space, then maybe we need to ask, who do I need to help? It could be someone very close to us. Has someone in our family lost their job? Can we offer a lending hand for a while? Maybe it is our child who needs help. Maybe it is our parents who are old now and need care.

Whoever it is this week, together let us open our eyes and ask, who can I help or who do I need to ask for help? Then we can all say together in faith, hope, and love that life is good and when we die it is great.

---

1. Adapted from a theme raised in *Celebration: An Ecumenical Worship Resource*, (Kansas City, MO: National Catholic Reporter Company, Inc., November, 2001) 501.

The End – Good Bye!

I have tomorrow's newspaper here and I thought it would be interesting to talk about its headline. Can everyone see tomorrow's newspaper headline? It reads, 'The end – good bye!' Can you imagine that tomorrow will be the end of the world? The end of everything we own, everything we have, and everything we are. Just think about it for a second. Gone ... the end. Good bye!

In today's reading we hear from the prophet Malachi, who proclaims that a day is coming like a blazing oven which will consume the proud and the evildoer. The Lord's fire will completely eliminate all evil. Even Jesus evokes strong images in the gospel of Luke, saying that the temple will be destroyed; false prophets will arise; there will be rumours of wars and insurrections; nation will rise against nation; there will be earthquakes, plagues, and famines; and there will a general persecution of all who remain faithful to the gospel of Jesus Christ. There will even be strife within families to the point of death. In other words, it will be the end. It would be like us receiving the headline 'The end – good bye!'

So how are we to react to such troubling or unsettling news?[1] Each of the three readings today gives us advice: Malachi suggests to fear the Lord. Paul counsels us to 'work quietly'. And Jesus bids us to not worry but remain faithful.

But let's look at this a little more carefully. Malachi says fear the name of the Lord and the sun will shine. Hang on a second, since when is fear a good thing? Well, we need to understand what this word really means in the language it was written, Hebrew. Here the word does not mean fear as in 'run and hide' but more 'to be in awe of'. Biblical fear is more to do with 'wonder and awe'. So we ought to marvel at the Lord's hand in our lives. Then Paul counsels us to work quietly. Here Paul is advising the community to remain faithful in the ordinary, everyday tasks of life. Some people in his time, believing that Jesus' return was imminent, gave up trying to live a faith-filled life and said, 'What's the point, it's too late! Let's live it up!' Paul rejects this attitude and encourages the community and us to be busy living the gospel, labouring for justice, freedom, and peace. And, of course, Jesus himself does not mince his words – he invites us to remain faithful always. In times of trial, he says, do not worry as he will be there to give us the right words and he will never abandon us in any way. He will give us courage to face all our trials. His Spirit will shine through our human limitations.

This really is all the same advice – we are called to remain faithful and live the gospel now. We are living the gospel by coming here. We are living the gospel by being neighbour to someone sick. We are living the gospel by forgiving others. We are living the gospel by being remaining faithful in marriage. We are living the gospel by being a good parent. We are living the gospel by loving one another.

So today is not 'the end – good bye!' Instead it is 'a new beginning – welcome!'

1. William F. Maestri, *Grace Upon Grace*, (Makati, Philippines: St Paul Publications, 1988) 320.

Our Lord Jesus Christ, Universal King
2 Sam 5:1-3; Col 1:12-20; Lk 23:35-43

Christ the King of Our Lives

I had a conversation with a friend of mine over Thanksgiving about evolution and the universe. He was telling me how large the universe was with its thousands of galaxies and millions of planets. There has to be another planet with intelligent life on it, he claimed, and thus there is no room for a God who creates us uniquely. Of course, as a priest, I objected and argued the existence of God. It was a great discussion and then he asked, 'What difference does Jesus make anyway?' I was caught off guard by the question and could not name one specific thing immediately except for Jesus makes all the difference. I said God is love itself and Christ is the exemplar of love. Christ makes all the difference because he is love itself.

The letter to the Colossians tells us that 'Christ is the image of the invisible God, the firstborn of all creation. For in him were created all things in heaven and earth, the visible and invisible, whether thrones or dominions or principalities or powers; all things were created through him and for him.' (Col 1:12)

In other words all creation is in him. He is the centre of all things created. Thus he is the king of creation. That is what we celebrate today in the Feast of Christ the King. The church celebrates this feast as the last Sunday of the liturgical calendar as a reminder of who is the centre of the universe – Christ.

This feast was established by Pope Pius XI at the beginning of the 1900s to remind all of humanity of the importance of Christ. With the demise throughout Europe of kings and queens as we knew them and the rise of a new way to govern, Pope Pius felt that there was a danger of losing the significance of the Christ event. So he established this feast as a reminder of the centrality of Christ to the universe.

Yes, we hear that Christ is the centre of all things created in the letter to the Colossians. Yet we also hear in the gospel today of Christ crucified on the cross. How are we to understand our king since he was crucified? How are we to reconcile these two seemingly irreconcilable statements? We need to look at Christ as our exemplar. We look to him for how to act in all things. And we see that even in his last moments Jesus loved as God, his

Father, had asked of him. He forgave and reconciled even in the pain and anguish of his dying moment. He loved even in the moment of pain and suffering.

We are called to love at all times, especially in times of pain and suffering. We are called to love always and that is not easy. We have all just celebrated Thanksgiving and spent time with family members. During this time we often realise that there are some family members who are easy to love and then there are others who are not so easy to love. Maybe it was the relative who was not invited to dinner. Maybe it was the relative who was invited but never came. Maybe it was the relative who came but was not invited. Whoever it was this season, there are people in our lives whom we can find hard to forgive or love. Today Christ is inviting us to forgive and love as he did on the cross. We are called to forgive and love especially in the tough times.

So as we close our liturgical year and start a new year we can take this opportunity to start anew. To recognise Christ the King in all our lives and forgive and love as Christ did, thus making Christ the King of our lives.